Hidden Government

Hidden Government

By

Lieut. Colonel J. Creagh Scott

The A.K. Chesterton Trust

2017

© The A.K. Chesterton Trust, BM Candour, London, WC1N 3XX, UK

Website: www.candour.org.uk

ISBN: 978-1-9122-58-00-0 (Paperback)
ISBN: 978-1-9122-58-01-7 (Hardback)

Four editions were published by the Britons Publishing Society between 1954 and 1968. This is the fifth edition, published in 2017.

"Ye shall know the truth, and the truth shall make you free."

"The struggle is against the evils of International Zionism and its twin weapons of International Finance and International Communism, the real menace to peace of which humanity is kept in complete ignorance."

(*The Spokesman*, New Zealand)

". . . . this world-wide conspiracy for the overthrow of civilisation and for the reconstitution of society on the basis of arrested development, of envious malevolence and impossible equality, has been steadily growing.. . . . .

There is no need to exaggerate the part played in the creation of Bolshevism and in the actual bringing about of the Russian Revolution by these international and for the most part atheistical Jews. It is certainly a very great one; it probably outweighs all others. With the notable exception of Lenin, the majority of the leading figures are Jews. Moreover the principal inspiration and driving power comes from Jewish leaders."

WINSTON CHURCHILL,

Illustrated Sunday Herald, 8th February, 1920

Lieut. Colonel John Creagh Scott c. 1900

CONTENTS

Photograph of the author 5

Dedication 8

Preface to the fifth edition 9

Introduction 13

I. Is there a Hidden Hand? 17

II. What is The Plan? 19

III. The Zionists and The Plan 32

IV. "Anti-Semitism" and The Plan 40

V. Palestine and The Plan 44

VI. State Control and The Plan 56

VII. The Money-Power and The Plan 64

VIII. Export and The Plan 67

IX. The Press and The Plan 72

X. Communism and The Plan 76

XI. Christianity and The Plan 84

XII. Is This the Anti-Christ? 99

Appendix 1. J Creagh Scott obituary from *Candour* 106

Suggested reading list 107

DEDICATED TO ALL MEN OF GOOD WILL

The contention of this book is that the amazing things bewildering and shattering the world to-day, are not haphazard, or the result of coincidence, or even of what is sometimes called " The onward march of events," but are the outcome of a Master Plan of human, or, as some may think, inhuman, agency; into which Plan this book probes, in the general interest and for the safety of The Realm.

Preface to the Fifth Edition.

John Creagh Scott was born on September 18th, 1879 in Killadysert, County Clare, Ireland. He was the first son of Mary and James Creagh Scott. From the age of 20 he was in active service with the Argyll and Sutherland Highlanders throughout the Boer War where he was eventually seriously wounded in action. During the First World War he commanded on the Somme with distinction and in addition to his numerous Mentions in Despatches of Sir Douglas Haig and Sir John French he also received the Croix de Guerre avec Etoile d'Or. He left the front line after a shell exploded just yards behind him. The blast riddled him with shrapnel, left him blind in one eye and deaf in one ear. This was the second time he had been wounded in the line of duty.

Though much of the information regarding his military career can be obtained with relative ease, digging any deeper into his political life after that time however has proved to be something of an enigma. It is my understanding that at this time there are still a great many documents and records still being kept hidden from the scrutiny of researchers that would prove most useful to this end. These are currently deemed "*too recent for release*" by MI5, Special Branch and the Home Office. Surely the activities of this man, born more than 130 years ago, cannot still be deemed a threat to the modern day establishment? ....can they?

"Jock" (as he was known by his close friends) had an unquenchable passion for fishing. It is well documented that salmon and trout culture were a lifelong fascination for him. At home in Moretonhampstead, Devon he spent countless hours crafting flies. He even owned a stretch of the river Exe and a stretch of the river Teign. One of the local train drivers would make an unscheduled stop 'a fields stroll' from one of his hidden stretches of waterway. On his return journey up the single track railway the driver would again stop and wait for the Colonel (a local nickname) to appear from the tree line and walk back across the field offering a share of his catch in return. Jocks passion for fishing was such that he even took a poacher's rod to France as part of his unofficial kit. One diary entry reads "Jerry all quiet, gone fishing" and later that same day "Jerry opened up, beat a hasty retreat!"

What he saw during the Boer war angered him deeply. He openly voiced in later years his distain toward the conduct and policies undertaken by the British at that time, especially when it was eventually realised who's interests the conflict had actually served. He was not the only one who had seen past the charade. His studies and indeed his circles of friends put him in close contact with a lot of like minded people many of whom were actively seeking to expose the truth and work towards the good of the common man. Upon the request of A. K. Chesterton, Jock also became active on behalf of the League of Empire Loyalists and *Candour*.

According to his youngest daughter, Jock *"was a gentle man who associated himself with anybody and on the other hand, threw lavish parties, especially at hogmanay and New Year when all the guests were either members of the elite and very much upper class in those days. He would dress up in his kilt and make a toast in Gaelic."*

Jock's book *Hidden Government* was the result of years of research and though much was done to discredit the Colonel and his book by the establishment at the time, (something he no doubt expected) *Hidden Government* still sold over 7,000 copies in the first year it was released. A determined fighter both on the battlefield and in the struggle for the rights of men!

While others were being protected and pulled out of danger before the battle of the Somme, it was Jock that stepped up to potentially take their place in the firing line. So it was in the battle against Zionism and International Finance also. He placed himself in the firing line because to him, it wasn't just a choice, it was a moral obligation. It's quite ironic however to note that had there been no-one else available to take over command of the 6th Battalion, Royal Scots Fusiliers at the time, 'temporary Lieutenant-Colonel' Churchill may not have made it back to England to cause as much trouble as he eventually did which may have saved the L.E.L. an awful lot of work in the long run.

Despite all the warnings left for us over the years by great men like Creagh Scott the global elite still keep managing to subvert the message and therefore the opinions of the masses. Through means of the internet and reprints such as the one you now hold in your hand, the message of truth will continue to be spread by those good men who decide it's their calling to do so. I would like to take this opportunity to offer my most heartfelt thanks to some of those very men for ensuring *Hidden Government* has been published once again. Colin Todd, whose selfless attitude has kept *Candour* in the field of battle (that alone would put a smile on Jocks face), Jez Turner who's interest and enthusiasm helped instigate the new release, Jeff Carson who bravely undertook the meticulous proof reading required for such a title, and the tireless efforts of Rob Black without whom this whole project would not have got off the ground.

The very idea that this authorised fifth edition of *Hidden Government* would be in your hands printed all crisp and fresh as a daisy in the 21st century, to me, is both a testament to the author's veracity and at the same time, a bitter pill to swallow. Seeing, as we have since then, how far things have progressed over the last 60 years in the same vein that Jock describes in this book.

Lieutenant Colonel John Creagh Scott D.S.O. O.B.E. died of

pneumonia at Langhill, Moretonhampstead, Devon on December 6th, 1957. He was 78 years old.

My Hero, my Grandfather.

Rest in Peace.

J. Mitchell
30th April 2017

Radley College, left 1894

INTRODUCTION

An open letter from the Author to You

DEAR READER

This is an objective study...
based on years of patient and thorough research by a body of public-spirited men...
representing a wide diversity of backgrounds, tastes, professions and pursuits...
bound together in one common purpose...
to find and reveal, if possible, the ultimate reason for the world's continuing unrest, strife and unhappiness...
a problem that concerns us all...
man, woman and child...
without exception...
deeply and intimately...
urgently and individually...
including you and your loved ones...
NOW!

* * *

Is the fundamental cause of all our world upset...
our wars and rumours of wars...
our want and poverty...
our restrictions and shortages...
the unspeakable miseries and sufferings of millions of our fellow humans all over the wide and bountiful earth, so eager and prodigal of giving...
the incessant carnage, destruction and devil's work all around us...
just a simple matter of economic maladministration to be righted by economic planning and theory...
on a world basis...

or a question of clashing ideologies and competing propagandas...
or is there something more sinister and mysterious...
more menacing...
more fruitful of further and continuing horror, degradation and terror...
behind and overshadowing all these agencies of evil...
something so obscene, so bestial, so unspeakably vile that it has no name but Satanism...
working relentlessly, secretly and ruthlessly through its chosen human agents...
for final and irrevocable victory in its age-old struggle for world mastery and the enslavement of the human soul and the degradation of the human body?

* * *

That is the problem that this book sets out to solve...
and one you cannot afford to ignore or neglect if you value your life, your liberty and your welfare, now and hereafter...
the most important problem before the world to-day...
what we must do to be saved from the merciless ones who seek our destruction, the high priests and eager agents of Satanism...
the anti-Christ...
to whom nothing is sacred and all is serviceable in its unending war for the overthrow of Christendom.

* * *

Read this book, then, with an open mind...
judging it solely by its message and not by any artificial standards or preconceived ideas...
that you may understand what has befallen you and yours...
is befalling and will continue to befall you...
unless you "take arms against a sea of troubles, And, by opposing, end them."
for, make no mistake about this, you are yourself the enemy of yourself and all you hold dear...

if, having acquainted yourself of the truth, you acquit the lie through indifference, complacence or mistaken tolerance...
for, as Burke said greatly, "the only thing necessary for the triumph of evil is that good men do nothing." Silence is crime.

> "Pray thee, take care, that tak'st my book in hand,
> To read it well; that is, to understand."

The Author,
Moretonhampstead,
January, 1954.
Devon.

ACKNOWLEDGEMENTS.

The author wishes to acknowledge with sincere thanks the valuable help he has received in preparing this book from The Judge Armstrong Foundation, B., G.W., R.E., C.H.J., F.B., J.G.O., S.W., K.P., and, in particular, from Mr. George Wilson for his aid in the revision and editing of the original script.

The Author.

I
IS THERE A HIDDEN HAND?

"Governments do not govern, but merely control the machinery of government, being themselves controlled by the hidden hand."
DISRAELI.

FIELD Marshal Smuts, statesman, scholar and soldier, not long before he died said: "I am sure there is some hidden pressure behind all the worries of Europe, Asia and America." If such a man was so convinced, the ordinary citizen may be forgiven if he finds himself increasingly bewildered and worried when he surveys what Winston Churchill calls "the darkening scene."

Well may we repeat the question now being asked on every hand by all types and classes of people, "What is behind all this trouble? Is there some sinister organisation that is engineering it for their own purpose? If so, who are they and what are those purposes? Who, in short, benefits?" For, obviously, unless somebody benefited from the devil's brew of world-wide trouble that is kept boiling and bubbling, there would be none. And indeed, well may it be asked why such men as Smuts and Churchill, with their unrivalled access to the inner councils and secrets of public affairs, are unwilling, or, may be reluctant to disclose the exact nature and identity of the "hidden pressure" causing the ferments, disorders and hostility with which humanity is plagued.

To find and expose for public judgement and swift retribution, the hidden hand that is the cause of our endless miseries and anxieties, is the aim and purpose of this book. It is to this end that we ask these questions:

(1) Is Bolshevism behind our troubles?

(2) Or ineptitude, inexperience and doctrinal stupidity on the part of individual governments, with their clashing schemes and ambitions?

(3) Or is it due simply and mostly to the "Old Adam" inherent in perverse human nature, as such?

(4) Is it "Imperialism," old or new, greedy, covetous and ruthless?

(5) Is it an "Armaments' Ring" or an international cartel, grasping for the wealth of the world in the terms of oil and gold and rubber and grain?

(6) Or is it something more cunning, more deadly and more powerful than any of these, deliberately exploiting them for its own sinister ends? In short, is it, indeed, "The Hidden Hand" and, if so, whose hand is it and how does it operate? Let us see.

Everywhere that the research work on this book led through the past several years it led sometimes directly and unmistakably, at other times by devious and hidden paths, but always to the same source and origin of the world's manifold troubles—namely, what has become known to millions of people all over the world as THE PLAN.

What and whose PLAN this is, how it operates and what its diabolical purpose is, will be made plain in the course of this book. Suffice it to say now that it clearly shows that there IS a Hidden Hand and whose hand it is.

For THE PLAN is the carefully designed instrument of the hand, created to serve it faithfully and unceasingly through time until it is fulfilled.

II

WHAT IS THE PLAN?

"There is some hidden pressure behind all the worries of Europe, Asia and America."

THE LATE FIELD-MARSHAL SMUTS.

THE world first learned of THE PLAN (which is drawn up in a series of Protocols) in 1905 when it fell into the hands of one, Sergyei Nilus, a Russian and probably a member of the Imperial Russian Secret Service, who published it. A copy of it was lodged with the British Museum the following year (1906). It is officially known as "The Protocols of the Learned Elders of Zion" and was obviously intended to be kept strictly secret.

It is not surprising, therefore, that it was promptly repudiated as "a forgery" by Jewry as a whole, and particularly by its authors. After all, its contents of conspiracy, to bear such bitter fruit in the Revolution, were not likely to endear them to the Government of the day. At that time, Jews were not exactly the spoiled darlings they later became under the Soviet regime.

Ever since that first publication, THE PLAN has been denounced as a "forgery" by the Jews concerned. But the question remains, "Is it?" It is the purpose of this book to examine that question in the light of the contents of THE PLAN itself, and the fact that they have proved to be uncannily accurate forecasts of what has been happening in the world for many years.

All quotations can be verified by reference to THE PLAN itself, copies of which can be obtained from the Publishers[1], The Britons

---

[1] The author was writing in 1954. Although the Britons no longer exist, this book is available freely available on the internet, as well as on many on-line

Publishing Society, 74, Princedale Road, London, W.11, and many leading booksellers.

Even during the comparatively moderate Kerensky regime, anyone found in Russia with a copy of THE PLAN was shot. Why? What happened under the much more brutal Bolshevists, from whom Kerensky fled, can well be imagined.

If THE PLAN is fraudulent, the Jewish governments that have been in power in Russia since the discovery and publication of this highly secret and sinister document have shown a determination to repudiate its genuineness that is most remarkable.

Even admitting its highly explosive nature, why should any Government show such sustained and venomous hostility over a spurious document? Why devote so large a portion of their time and substance to pursuing a phantom?

Fifty years are surely enough for experts in Jewish religion and literature to be able to convince a sympathetic world of the inherent falsity of THE PLAN from its own form and substance if it IS an impudent and mischievous forgery? Surely it is not beyond the vaunted genius of the Jews to subject THE PLAN to the same expert examination that all suspect documents of public importance are subjected to, when they first solicit public patronage as works of genuine worth; and then to submit their own proofs of forgery to independent official check?

Why were not such steps taken long ago? Because the alleged forgery was not of sufficient importance to warrant any such scrutiny on behalf of the good name of Jewry as a whole? If so, why the repeated and insistent repudiation? In short, why spend time and energy, as the Zionists do, denouncing THE PLAN when its authenticity could be discredited for all time by proving it to be a forgery by the orthodox

bookseller platforms. [RB]

and infallible methods employed by the great museums and libraries when asked to decide the authenticity of important scripts?

These doubts cloud the public mind concerning the sincerity of the repudiation. It cannot therefore be surprising if the public prefer to regard THE PLAN as genuine and the cry of "forgery" as false, in view of the nature of THE PLAN itself and in the light of how it is being steadily carried out to the danger of world peace and individual liberty and happiness.

That is why THE PLAN must be studied and understood by the ordinary public for what it is—a vast conspiracy against the security and welfare of all other nations and peoples. It is not sufficient for Zionism to answer so serious a charge with typical Jewish clamour about "forgeries" and "Jew-baiting" and "anti-Semitism." The matter and times are too grave for those hackneyed defences to be of avail. If the charges are false it should not be difficult for Zionists to prove them so. It is certainly in their best interests to do so without further delay or evasion, if they can.

Then there is the judgement of the Court at Berne, Switzerland, which sustained the Jewish claim. Unaware of what followed, well-meaning people hug it to their bosoms.

The case came before a Court of Appeal which reversed the decision of the Appellate Court saying that the evidence utterly failed to establish the Jewish claim. The final judgement, therefore, acquitted the defendants of the charge of libel by publication and distribution of THE PLAN and inferentially established its authenticity.

In addition there is the word of a well-known Jewish lawyer of New York, Henry Klein[2], who with courageous honesty has said openly

---

[2] Henry H. Klein (1879 - 1955) was an anti-Communist and anti-Zionist Jewish attorney. He defended pro bono Christian patriots charged with sedition in the famous "Sedition" Show Trial of 1942-1944. [RB]

that THE PLAN is in fact the "World Plot of the Jewish Sanhedrin." Writing in *Women's Voice* (Chicago) in 1945, he said; "The Protocols (i.e. THE PLAN for World Domination) are both true and authentic, and the heads of World Zionism compose The Grand Sanhedrin which desires world control." He added as a sequel "The Jews have driven me from the tribe because I have denounced their sinister plans."

There was held at Basle in 1897 what was called a "Zionist Convention." It was attended, not only by Zionists from all over the world, but by Russian Secret Police.

The Czarist Police arranged for a fire in the building on the second or third day of the Convention. The Jews fled, the police rushed in, seized whatever papers they could lay hands on and returned with them to Moscow. Amongst the papers, according to Norman Thompson, in his *Origin and Scientific Solution of the Economic World Chaos*, were drafts of THE PLAN. All copies were destroyed during the Kerensky regime, and thereafter the possession of them was punishable by death. Victor Marsdon, Russian correspondent of *The Morning Post* however, procured a copy, and upon his return to London translated it into English.

The *Morning Post* disclosed THE PLAN, and it was reported that certain advertisers and others withdrew their patronage soon afterwards. In any case, it was not long before *The Post* ceased independent publication.

Writing of this Zionist Convention at Basle in 1897, Judge Armstrong of Texas says, in his famous book called *Traitors*, published in 1948:

"The scheme for a League of Nations and later U.N.O. and a resultant Zionist World Empire was hatched at the Zionist Convention at Basle in 1897.... The Zionists there proclaimed their purpose to subjugate the Christian people of the world and to establish a Zionist Empire with their king as ruler. THE PLAN reveals their plan of conquest. They boast that with few negligible exceptions, they then controlled the Press and gold of the world."

Nor would it appear that either his title or his language is too strong, if we consider the following statement from THE PLAN itself:

"The weapons in our hands are limitless ambitions, burning greediness, merciless vengeance, hatred and malice."

(You will find that gem of candour and charity in Protocol 9 of THE PLAN.) For further evidence of the nature of THE PLAN, consider these extracts, which can he found in the respective Protocols numbered below:

"We have got our hands into the administration of the law, into the conduct of elections, into the Press." Protocol 14.

"Freedom is the right to do that which the law allows... all freedom will be in our hands, since the laws will abolish or create only that which is desirable for us." Protocol 12.

"Our counter-sign is force and make-believe." Protocol 1.

"It will be no disgrace to be a spy and informer, but a merit... in our plan one third will keep the rest under observation from a sense of duty, on the principle of volunteer service to the State." Protocol 17.

"There remains a small space to cross and the whole long path we have trodden is ready now to close its cycle of the symbolic snake, by which we symbolise our people. When the ring closes all the States of Europe will be locked as in a powerful vice." Protocol 3.

"The Press is entirely in our hands." Protocol 7.

"Literature and journalism are two of the most important educative forces, and therefore our government will become the proprietor of the majority of the journals." Protocol 12.

"Our kingdom will be an apologia of the divinity of Vishnu, in whom is found its personification. In our hundred hands will be, one in each, the springs of the machinery of social life." Protocol 17

"...Force makes no terms with any right, not even with that of God." Protocol 22.

"What I am about to set forth is our system from the two points of view, that of ourselves, and that of the Goyim, i.e. non-Jews... the best results in government are attained in violence and terrorisation..." Protocol 1.

"Our right lies in force." Protocol 1.

"To us Jews it should be plain to see what a disintegrating importance Communism has upon the minds of the Goyim." Protocol 2.

"All the fields of the machinery of all the States go by force of the engine, which is in our hands, and that engine is—gold." Protocol 5.

"The people have raised a howl about the necessity of settling the question of Socialism by way of international agreement. Division into parties has given them into our hands, for, in order to carry on a contested struggle one must have money, and the money is all in our hands..."

"In this way the blind force of the people remains our support and we—and we only—shall provide them with a leader and, of course, direct them along the road that leads to our goal." Protocol 9.

"What do we care if the ranks of those striving for power should be thinned, if there should arise a deadlock... a deadlock which will finally disorganise the country?" Protocol 10.

"The daily need for bread forces the Goyim to keep silence and be our humble servants." Protocol 13

"... Our orators will expound great problems which have turned humanity upside down in order to bring it at the end under our beneficent rule." Protocol 15.

Even with these few precepts, taken at random from THE PLAN itself, as a guide, it becomes comparatively easy to understand much that was puzzling before. Now can be seen the nature of the satanic stratagem for world domination going on in our midst, constituting mental manipulation operating through Church and State, entirely unsuspected and therefore unbelievable.

In the light of this revelation can now be better understood the seemingly disconnected sequence of events and circumstances connected with the two World Wars, the League of Nations, Dumbarton Oaks, Bretton Woods, the San Francisco Conference, the "New Deal," recent legislation in Britain aiming at the gradual elimination of individual initiative and responsibility, nationalisation of Industry accompanied by debt, the deprival of the right of the individual to contract out and forced to submit to compulsion, and the division of Germany containing the explosive ingredients of a third World War.

For even clearer understanding of the real cause of the manifold troubles that beset us to-day, driving us ruthlessly into the abyss of destruction and despair, ponder these revealing " NOTES " which are culled from the Foreword of THE PLAN itself—a PLAN which was first formulated as far back as the 9th Century B.C., by Solomon and other Jewish leaders, as a scheme for the conquest of the then known world by means other than the expensive and dangerous ones of open war.

Extracts from "The Notes":

"These learned men... with the slyness of the Symbolic Snake, whose head was to represent those who have been initiated in the plans of the

Jewish administration, and the body of the snake to represent the Jewish people. As the snake penetrated into the hearts of nations... it undermined and devoured all the non-Jewish power of these States... It is foretold that the snake has still to finish its work, until the return of its head to Zion, until the snake has completed its round of Europe, and encompassed the whole world. Thus it aims to accomplish the objective by using every endeavour to subdue other countries by economical conquest. A map of the course of the snake is shown as follows:

1st. stage. In 429 B.C. in Greece where - at the time of Pericles —the snake started eating into the power of that country.

2nd stage. About 69 B.C. in Rome in the time of Augustus.

3rd stage. A.D. 1552 in Madrid. (The Inquisition).

4th stage. About 1790 in Paris. (The French Revolution).

5th stage. In London from 1814 onwards.

6th stage. In Berlin from 1871 onwards. (The Prussian menace).

7th stage. In St. Petersburg over which is drawn the head of the snake under the date 1881.

8th stage. 1905 in Russia onwards. (The 1917 Revolution).

"All these States which the snake has traversed have had the foundations of their constitutions shaken. Arrows indicate the head of the snake moving on to Moscow, Kieff and Odessa. (It is well known to what extent the latter cities are centres of militant Jewry)."

9th stage. Constantinople to Jerusalem. (Palestine).

This map was drawn years before the occurrence of the Young Turk (i.e. Jewish) Revolution in Turkey. (Nilus of Russia in his Epilogue to the 1905 edition of THE PLAN).

Note that when the head of the snake reaches its tail in Palestine the conquest of Europe by Judaic-Communism will be approaching its objective. Consider what happened in Palestine!

THE PLAN has been discredited as a "forgery," though how a plan which has materialised in such detail can be a forgery would challenge considerable ingenuity to explain.

As witness the following significant incidents and events all of which seem to be too apt to be just coincidental:

1. The release of the Jew Bronstein better known as "Trotsky" from arrest in Halifax, Nova Scotia, when on his way to have millions of helpless Russians butchered. (1917).

2. The suppression by the British Foreign Office of the vital passage in the report on Bolshevism of Netherlands Minister Oudendyk, representative of The Netherlands Government at St. Petersburg when the reign of Bolshevist terror began. This passage reads as follows: "The danger is now so great that I feel it my duty to call the attention of the British and all other Governments to the fact that, if an end is not put to Bolshevism at once, the civilisation of the whole world will be threatened. This is not an exaggeration, but a sober fact. I consider that the immediate suppression of Bolshevism is the greatest issue now before the world, not even excluding the war still raging, and unless, as above stated, Bolshevism is nipped in the bud immediately, it is bound to spread in one form or another over Europe and the whole world, as it is organised and worked by Jews who have no nationality, and whose object is to destroy for their own ends the existing order of things. The only manner in which this danger can be averted would be collective action on the part of all the Powers."

The above passage was contained in a British White Paper and issued by the War Cabinet in April, 1919. It was subsequently removed from circulation and became officially unobtainable. A later edition appeared with the passage by Oudendyk removed.

One is forced to ask why the original White Paper was suppressed, by whose authority, and for what purpose? Is there, indeed, "A Hidden Hand," a Government within Government?

3. "The Balfour Declaration."

4. Berlin made an island in a Russian Bolshevist ocean.

5. The Nuremberg Trials.

It is therefore clear that the details of THE PLAN dovetail too closely into those of world events and legislation to be merely a fantasy or forgery. Those most concerned with THE PLAN have denied authorship, but world events confute them. Its most striking characteristic is seen in the shape of things not only to come BUT WHICH HAVE COME, unless the ordinary people rise up and assume their right of personal initiative and indeed, their right to self-preservation. Until then, to look for escape from the frustrations all around is to look for a miracle of grace. Consider these further excerpts from various Protocols, if still in doubt.

(a) "Our right lies in force. The word right is abstract thought and proved by nothing. The word means no more than; give me what I want in order that thereby I may have a proof that I am stronger than you." Protocol 1.

(b) "We have included in the constitution such rights as to the masses appear fictitious and not actual rights. All these so-called 'Peoples Rights' can exist only in idea." Protocol 3.

(c) "From the premier dictators of the present day the Goyim suffer patiently and bear such abuses as, for the least of them, they would have beheaded twenty kings." Protocol 3.

(d) "Dictators whisper to the peoples through their agents that they are inflicting injury on the states with the highest purpose—to secure the welfare of the peoples. Naturally they do not tell the peoples that this unification 'must be accomplished under our sovereign rule... thanks to this state of things the peoples are destroying every kind of stability and creating disorders at every step." Protocol 3.

(e) "Putting aside fine phrases we shall speak of the significance of each thought; by comparisons and deductions we shall throw light on surrounding facts... OUR system from the two points of view, that of ourselves and that of the Goyim, that is non-Jews." Protocol I.

(The word "Goyim" or "Goy" is a Jewish term meaning cattle or non-Jews. It is used throughout THE PLAN).

The clue to how all this is accomplished is suggested by Douglas Reed in his well-known work *From Smoke to Smother*, where, talking of the mass hypnotism technique, he says: "The bludgeoning and intimidatory effect of mass-propaganda on the mass-mind is staggering."

It should now be clear to even the most obtuse and sceptical amongst us, that some super world force or government is at work in the world's affairs; and whether we prefer to call it Satanism, or the anti-Christ, or just the plain old-fashioned devil, it operates coldly, ruthlessly, secretly and unceasingly according to some plan in its onward relentless march towards its goal of world dictatorship. Furthermore, it will be seen that the policy of THE PLAN is now reaching its zenith. The supreme test is approaching. It has to be decided, whether human life is to be centrally, controlled by, a supreme political and economic world dictatorship, or by the operation of man's free-will, in accordance with the precepts of natural law.

THE PLAN reveals the hidden purpose, the establishment of Judaic world domination. It explains in brazen detail the methods to be employed, and that are being employed, now, with effect, for securing domination over all peoples.

Looking round the world, (but one need not look beyond one's own borders), the people should be able to see what regimentation and political promises mean. They mean; "We promise some of you Paradise—but all of you, eventually, will get hell!"

That is the gospel according to Karl Marx, the Jew—German—Polish—Russian, professional agitator, nihilist revolutionist, conscienceless social parasite and flagrant plagiarist. His notorious *Das Kapital*, which he compiled in the British Museum, under the protecting wing of this country to which he had fled with the French Security Police at his heels, was merely the prototype of Judaic-Communism as set forth in THE PLAN. But perhaps *Das Kapital* is only a forgery also![3]

Both are atheistic and grossly materialistic, rejecting all concepts of moral law and denying the inviolate rights of humanity, while, of course enjoying and insisting on the benefits of both.

We should reject the authenticity of THE PLAN at our peril, for the doubtful satisfaction of joining in the parrot-cry of "forgery" might well prove to be our swan-song as a nation. For God's law, the law of nature, cannot be violated with impugnity.

It is within our reach and power to right this satanic wrong that is being deliberately, fiendishly and incessantly done to us and mankind, by destroying THE PLAN before it destroys us and our loved ones and our Country, as well as, bit by bit, civilisation itself. The most powerful admonition and weapon for its protection ever placed in the

---

[3] Karl Marx wrote about Kapital, calling his book *Das Kapital*. Nowhere has he attempted to define the meaning of the title of his book.

hand of humanity is "Ye shall know the Truth and the Truth shall make you free."

But only if the Truth is understood and acted upon, not merely known and left at that. The admonition implies an universal, resolute change of outlook without which there can be no material change, for all political parties, wholly or in part, come within the orbit of THE PLAN.

YOU are therefore confronted with vital decisions. NOW!

III

THE ZIONISTS AND THE PLAN

"We have made a gulf between the far-seeing Sovereign Power and the blind force of the people, so that both have lost their meaning. For like the blind man and his stick, both are powerless. To-day I may tell you that our goal is now only a few steps off. There remains a small space to cross, and the whole long path we have trodden is ready now to close its cycle of the Symbolic Snake, by which we symbolise our people. When this ring closes all the states of Europe will be locked in its coils, as in a powerful vice."

PROTOCOL 3.

ZIONISM is the militant branch of world-wide Jewry and is therefore their instrument for world subjugation. Masquerading behind a pseudo-religious name, designed to allay suspicion and, indeed, arouse sympathy and support among Christians ignorant of its true nature and objects, Zionism pretends to be concerned only with the establishment of a "Homeland" for the poor scattered and "homeless" Jews of the world. Only that.

Which cunning plea might have greater substance were the truth not known that the "Zionists" are fanatically committed to the establishment of a world-empire with Palestine as its centre. From that fact radiates all the agitation, conspiracy and ferment that have bedevilled the racked world for the past fifty years.

However, all Jews are not "Zionists." A rift in the ranks of Judaism has begun. Thus, we read, that just before the end of World War Two —or at any rate, the breathing space we are now being given before the next lot—in the city of Houston, Texas, a protest meeting was held by the "Reformed Jews," and they were promptly denounced as "traitors" by the "Zionists," led by their High Priest, Rabbi Wise of New York, arch-agitator for the "Zionists" and their schemes, apologist for their deeds, however revolting to unbiased onlookers.

So we see, there are really two types of Jews—the political "Zionists," relentless and militant conspirators against the world's peace and for the world's mastery—and those Jews who oppose their excesses.

They see in the British Commonwealth a world power based on decentralisation, and therefore in direct opposition to their conception of world power based on rigorous centralisation. So they use the doctrine of Communism which has been spread through schools and youth organisations to undermine the youth of the nation, using them in turn to undermine the British Commonwealth and the British way of life. It has been remarked that the characteristics of the British people have undergone a lamentable change since the war, amounting to character degradation.

They see in the idea of world organisation, like the League of Nations and U.N.O. a further opportunity and means of gaining their goal of World Mastery. Thus, we have the President of the "Zionist Congress" boasting that "The League of Nations is a Jewish idea." Well might he so boast, since only the year before, speaking at Copenhagen in 1931, the well-meaning Professor Arnold Toynbee[4] let the cat out of the bag when he said in his official capacity as Secretary of the Royal Institute of International Affairs whose headquarters are at historic Chatham House; "The League of Nations as contemplated postulated the undermining of the sovereignty of our respective nations."

---

[4] Arnold Joseph Toynbee (1889 – 1975) was a British historian, philosopher of history, research professor of international history at the London School of Economics and the University of London and author of numerous books. He was regarded as a leading specialist on international affairs between 1918 and 1950). [RB]

Upon which rapturous declaration it would be difficult to concoct a more cogent comment than that of the eminent Social Creditor, the late C. H. Douglas, when he remarked; "The underlying meaning of this is so important that a little space is needed to deal with it. The ostensible reason for the League of Nations is the abolition of force as a means of settling disputes. But it is essential to notice that the advocates of the abolition of the use of force by nations assume that the exercise of force by institutions upon individuals is natural, lawful and ought to be extended. That is to say, there is no suggestion that the sovereignty of a government over its citizens should be decreased. If one nation has a grievance against another, that is a matter to be settled by negotiation, as between equals; but if a tax, or any other decree, national or local, is imposed upon an individual, it is imposed and paid under the threat of overwhelming force.

The 'undermining of national sovereignty' of which Professor Toynbee is so proud, means simply that omnipotent institutions are removed further from the control of individuals as such, until, for him, their decrees, however harsh and oppressive, leave no possibility of appeal.

Thus, the national sovereignty of all other nations is to be destroyed so that, upon their ruins, the Zionists in accordance with THE PLAN, may rear the monstrous edifice of their own world government.

A pretty scheme, indeed, you may well think, but thoroughly unlikely; until you stop to think how insidious can be the appeal to mankind's yearning for brotherhood and peace—a noble yearning that is being cunningly exploited by the Zionists working through idealistic bodies like the League of Nations and the more innocent starry-eyed Toynbees such bodies attract. Nor is that the worst aspect of this foul conspiracy against human happiness, freedom and dignity. There is one that actually plumbs even lower depths—the corruption of the human soul. How otherwise can you account for this remarkable confession by the same Professor Toynbee, when he remarks, however naively: "We are doing with our hands what we deny with our lips"?

Such a remark makes one almost despair of human hope in the emergence of the human race from the abysmal night of its own self-deception. For while there is a plentiful supply of fools, there must be at least an equal supply of knaves to exploit them!

Suffice it now to quote their own words from the third Protocol:

"Far back in ancient times we were the first to cry among the masses of the people the words 'Liberty, Equality, Fraternity,' words many times repeated since those days, by stupid poll-parrots who...did not see that in nature there is no equality, cannot be freedom: that nature herself has established inequality of minds, of characters, and capacities...In all corners of the earth the words 'Liberty, Equality, Fraternity' brought to our ranks, thanks to our blind agents, whole legions who bore our banners with enthusiasm. And all the time these words were cankerworms at work boring into the well-being of the Goyim, putting an end everywhere to peace, quiet, solidarity, and destroying all the foundations of the Goya State."

Surely this cynical boasting, pregnant with diabolical intent, should lay to rest any doubts that may remain in an unbiased mind concerning the pressing and overwhelming danger that confronts us as individuals and as a race? For here is the very root of ruin for us as a people or as members of a community.

What more insidious or destructive influence could be spread amongst us than the perversion of values and standards whereby "liberty" becomes revolt against discipline; "equality" a stupid denial of obvious divergent human qualities and the immutable laws governing all forms of animal life, especially mankind; and "fraternity" becomes the shibboleth of the self-seeker and social parasite?

Surely nothing more is needed to adorn the sorry tale? Well, for good measure let us cull still another fragrant bloom from this devil's lush garden of deceit and conspiracy. In the Third Protocol we read these candid words about freedom itself:

"The word 'freedom' brings out the communities of men to fight against every kind of force, even against every kind of authority, even against God and the laws of nature. For this reason we, when we come into our kingdom, shall have to erase this word from the lexicon of life."

Yet we are supposed to have fought two world wars for Freedom! Twice within living memory we saved civilisation by our exertions and our example. For what? Because "the nations cannot come to even an inconsiderable private agreement without our secretly having a hand in it," says Protocol Five!

No wonder the United Nations spends its time in endless and barren argument and has already become merely a sounding board of abuse by the Zionists speaking through the mouth of the Kremlin. We do not need to ponder the meaning of the prolonged delays in arriving at even minor decisions, hastily abandoned almost as soon as reached under the ceaseless bickering, nagging and oriental abuse characteristic of the Zionists. No longer need we read into these obstructions some cunning plot on the part of Russia to gain time while she feverishly prepares for open war. For the same Protocol 5 kindly tells us all in the following plain words:

"We shall so wear down the Goyim that they will be compelled to offer us international power that will enable us without violence to absorb all the State forces of the world and to form a super-government." [5]

---

[5] Beginning with Federal European Government cherished by Churchill, et alia!

In the light of this, is it not now easy to understand the whole technique and tactic of the "cold war," as exemplified by the Berlin Blockade? In the light of these words taken from the Seventh Protocol, "Throughout all Europe, in other countries also, we must create ferments, disorders and hostility," is it not easy to understand the reason for Korea, Malaya, Egypt, Tibet, Persia, India and all the other trouble spots that have plagued us like Job's boils since we foolishly saved our tormentors once again?

They see in the Trades Unions a happy medium for their propaganda and plots which have almost disrupted the entire Trade Union movement. Fortunately, the T.U.C. woke up in sufficient time to condemn, and to some extent to outlaw, the more blatant forms of Communistic sabotage in their midst.

Unfortunately, the Unions are still ignorant of the far more dangerous elements still operating among and through them. Until they become aware of the identity and true purpose of these elements, they will continue to be a hot-bed of dissonance and strife in the national life, instead of what they were originally formed to be, a negotiating body on behalf of their members in industrial and business life.

Not until the T.U.C. learns and declares the truth about the moral, social and economic sabotage coldly practised in their name and under their protection at the instigation of the Zionists, can the Unions rise to their full stature of dignity and influence as the third pillar of the State. At present they are, in the workings of THE PLAN, merely the political blackmailers for their unseen but omnipresent Zionist masters. Which, if the ordinary rank and file of the Union Members, decent, law-abiding men, for the most part, but knew, they would soon put "paid" to that account! But until they do know the truth which will set them free once more, they will continue to carry out the directives of THE PLAN along the dangerous lines secretly laid out for them.

Zionists see in the ordinary peoples of the earth their best chance of success by playing upon their miseries, their appetites and their desires; by stirring up strife and accentuating grievances. This they can do easily because they have agents everywhere. For, says Protocol 5:

"The nations cannot come to even an inconsiderable private agreement without our secretly having a hand in it."

Furthermore, the work of their secret agents is made easier by encouraging the natural apathy of most people in political affairs. By their very indifference and inaction, the ordinary masses unknowingly forge the chains of their own enslavement, as laid down in THE PLAN. The power behind Zionist Militancy resides, strange as it may seem, in dispersion. Protocol 11 declaims:

"God has granted to us, his chosen people, the gift of dispersion, and in this which appears in all eyes to be our weakness, has come forth all our strength, which has now brought us to the threshold of sovereignty over all the world."

Nothing could be written explaining more clearly the militant nature of Zionism which uses its non-national status throughout the nations to gain control.

On every side, their bewildered peoples are asking for guidance and enlightenment. On every side one hears the question; "What can be the reason for so much trouble?" No one trouble is itself a cause, but an effect. The cause is clear enough if the nature of THE PLAN is understood, if it can be seen how men and women—Jews and non-Jews—are being "handled" by satanic influences leading them to self-destruction. We are rapidly becoming the ostriches of doom, in our individual and national drifting, bemused and benumbed. This drift in place of determination is the very essence of the conspiracy to keep us in thrall.

Ask yourself: who are the rulers of Russia? According to *The Defender*, published in Kansas, U.S.A., the Central Committee of the Communist Party in Moscow (1936) (the centre of International Communism) consisted of 59 men. 56 were Jews and the other 3 married Jewesses. At that time 14 ambassadors (including those appointed to Gt. Britain and the U.S.A.) were Jews. After the 1917 revolution in Russia those appointed to govern the Russian people, 25 in number, were all Jews but one, Lenin, who was a Russian. All changed their names to Russian ones. For example: Bronstein became Trotzky, Apfelbaum became Zinovieff, Steinman became Maisky. (*The Rulers of Russia* by The Rev. Denis Fahey).

We are entering upon Armageddon's final act. We have seen the first and second acts in the two world wars. The curtain is rising slowly but surely on the climax, seen in the "cold war" with the threat of another world war hanging over us. For what purpose? The men in the Kremlin, operating through their chosen medium, are reaching out for world domination and the slavery of the human race to Judaic communism.[6]

Whatever may be the reason for recent purges in Russia it can be discounted. The leopard cannot change his spots—neither can dictators afford to change established policy.

We are more than mere mutes before the act. We are, consciously or unconsciously, in one camp or the other. Let us take our places now—Christians or Zionists—on either side of the stage and prepare to play our respective parts.

---

[6] There is no such thing as Christian communism.

IV

"ANTI-SEMITISM" AND THE PLAN

"Anti-Semitism is indispensable to us for the management of our lesser brethren."

PROTOCOL 9.

THE cry of "anti-Semitism" is the stock-in trade of the Zionist. It is at once his chief defence and his closest consolation. It has become his "badge of suffering" which he proudly wears like a medal. Whenever he needs or wishes to excuse his conduct or explain to himself his unpopularity with Gentiles, he murmurs to himself, or screams to the world, the charge of "anti-Semitism". For, being a Jew, it would never occur to him that he, himself, might be the offending party.

Before going on with our examination into the tortuous workings of THE PLAN, particularly in its specific provisions for so-called anti-Semitism, let us examine this fond Jewish belief, for if it be true that the Jew's notorious unpopularity is due entirely, or even in large part, to racial or religious prejudice, then the vast non-Jewish portions of the world's peoples, Moslem, Christian, Buddhist, to say nothing about the many other non-Jewish religions and their myriad followers, are indeed guilty, of a deep and repulsive wrong and in deserved condemnation at the bar of history.

But are they? It is quite easy to determine and moreover both personal and provable. Ask yourself this question: "Why do I dislike Jews?" Whatever answer you may give to that question, the very last one will certainly be that it has anything to do with their religion, for the simple and sufficient reason that you don't even know what their religion is!

However, if you happen to be one of those superior persons who pretend you don't dislike Jews, pose the question, in fairness to Jews in general—how many people who do dislike them know anything about their religion? The whole contention is nonsense; and the amazing thing is that the belief is so wide-spread. But then, as Shaw was forever telling us relative to his absurd claim to be a better playwright than Shakespeare, that if we repeat something, even the most outrageous lie, sufficiently often, in time people will accept it as true and you as a wise man for telling it.

No, the reason for the unmistakable unpopularity of Jews has nothing to do with their religion. It arises from something much more prosaic, namely their habits and manners rooted in their self-torturing inferiority complex and their insistence on parading it in public, to the intense dislike and offence of the unwilling onlookers. That is the basic cause of what they like to think of as "anti-Semitism."

Nor need they or their befuddled non-Jew apologists—neurotics thinking with their emotions and mostly incapable of objective analysis; the sort of half-wits suffering from what has been admirably called "the Brumas Complex"!—fall back on the ancient and exploded myth of "anti-Semitism" arising solely or even at all from the Crucifixion. For dislike of Jews is as pronounced and much more deadly and open among non-Christian races than it is among those who profess to follow Christ. Furthermore and more especially, it is chiefly to be found among those races, like the Arabs, who have had to live near or with Jews for centuries—surely ample time to acquire admiration for the lovable qualities which sentimentalists try to persuade us are preponderant in the Jewish make up!—and who are themselves members of the Semitic race!

Please note that last remark particularly. Jews are not the only people who are entitled to be called "Semitic"; it is sheer arrogance on their part to appropriate the word as synonymous with themselves. Arabs are also Semitic, and few who loathe Jews even dislike Arabs. On the contrary, even when we have fought against Arabs, we have admired and liked them for the very qualities that are so singularly missing in the Jew and whose lack are an ever-present invitation for distrust and dislike. This very fact blows sky-high the other half of Jewish explanation of the universal detestation in which they are held by all other races, tribes and peoples, namely that it is racial in origin. It is nothing of the sort. It is personal, for the reasons stated above.

However, so that there should be no doubt on anyone's part as to why we have analysed this problem at such length—for neither this book nor this chapter is a catalogue of the too well-known Jewish failings, which, frankly, are not of sufficient concern or moment to bother listing—just glance at the heading to this chapter and let us see what our would-be masters, are doing with this phenomenon.

In Protocol 9 we read:

"If any States raise a protest against us it is only 'pro forma' at our discretion and by our direction, for their anti-semitism is indispensable to us for the management of our lesser brethren."

Which directive is pointed by the following informative and enlightening incident. *In My Time* (Huddlestone) the author writes: "Just before Hitler came to power I spent the winter in the south of France, in the midst of Jewish friends, with whom I took coffee every day on a terrace overlooking the Mediterranean. One day a Jewish leader in our Party said reflectively, When Hitler comes to power I hope he will persecute the Jews.' He went on to explain that after many centuries the Jewish race, despite its fecundity, only counted sixteen millions owing to assimilation, and persecution was necessary to revive the needed race consciousness. Arguments could not make him shift his ground. He hoped for persecution." Well, he got it, and the world knows what great propaganda Jewry has made of Hitler's "persecution of the Jews."

While on the subject of "persecution," it might be just as well to glance at the other side of the balance sheet for a moment and learn that all "persecutions" have not been at the expense of the Jews. They have managed to do quite a bit that way themselves, in between wailing sessions and organising cries of "Jew-baiting." In this connection, the extract below is most timely—and illuminating:

"Any assessments throughout the centuries of persecution of and by Jews must of course show a big excess of the *latter*, for Jewry by its imposition of its financial system and methods on the Gentile races has been the continuous cause of their economic poverty and misery, as well as of the wars and revolutions resulting from them." (*Patrons and Partisans of Usury*. Thompson.)

So, let us not be over-hasty in playing into the hands of those who would exploit our natural sympathy for suffering, our abhorrence of cruelty and our national insistence on tolerance and fair-play, for by so doing, we strengthen the very things we seek to abolish. Let us view dispassionately and where possible, impersonally, what lies behind all this out-cry about so-called anti-Semitism. What is the reason for it and what is its real purpose? Is it what it seems to be, merely the outraged cry of persecuted people or is it a cunning device to forestall criticism and prevent discovery? Most of all, is it deliberately provoked for the evil objects outlined in THE PLAN?

It is not the first time that such a use was made of humanity for inhuman ends. History is full of such instances, Russia providing the most recent and vivid example. There is nothing therefore in this regard in THE PLAN that need be dismissed as unlikely much less impossible. Rather is there much that demands urgent and close scrutiny lest we are being inveigled into exchanging our birthright of sturdy common sense for a mess of pottage of false sentiment.

Charity still begins at home!

V

PALESTINE AND THE PLAN

"Our countersign is force and make-believe."

TO understand the true significance of Palestine in relation to the Zionist master prototype for world conquest and exploitation, officially known as "THE PLAN," it is necessary to recall much that the Zionists would like forgotten. For instance, their "rights" to Palestine at all; their astounding methods in obtaining those "rights"; and, finally, their real reason for wanting and insisting on getting Palestine, in preference to other and more attractive places offered them as "a National Home."

When Great Britain shouldered the heavy burden of accepting the Palestine Mandate on behalf of the League of Nations after the First World War, and after she, by her sacrifice and exertions, with the limited but loyal aid of the Arabs under the fabulous Lawrence of Arabia, had freed Palestine from the barbarous yoke of the old Sultan of Turkey, they speedily discovered that, under one pretext or another, Palestine was being used as a dumping ground for the riff-raff from the ghettos of Europe; much to the alarm and impoverishment, as well as inconvenience and dislike, of the Arabs who had lived their pastoral lives there for over two thousand years.

When the Arabs rose in their wrath to drive out these alien intruders who were despoiling them of homes and livelihoods, the Zionists immediately set their machinery in motion. Wailing and agitation arose in every quarter likely to be of any help. Men and money were mobilised to flood the Christian countries with nauseating and misleading propaganda picturing these exploiters of the Arabs as the usual "poor, ill-treated, bewildered Jews once again being brutally abused by cruel oppressors." Mass meetings of hysterical Jews, led by their Zionist padrones, were organised in every large city here and in America. Thus we had the spectacle of the late Lord Melchett roaring from the platform of the Albert Hall: "The first duty of a Government is to govern." Meaning, of course, that once more, British treasure and lives were to be poured out to save Jews from the consequence of their own greed and unpopularity—and all in the name of law and order. (What a pity that some Christian politician didn't thunder Melchett's dictum from the same platform when a cowardly Government was allowing British troops to be murdered with impunity by these same Jews after the second world war!)

So once again The Zionists had their way and Great Britain had to bear the odium of having betrayed her own faithful Arab allies to whom she had pledged the security of Palestine as a reward for their assistance in the First World War—and all because of frenzied clamour engineered by The Zionists in every Christian country, and particularly in the United States, hot-bed of Jewish intrigue and propaganda.

How ironically history was to comment upon this shameful deed when, some twenty-five years later, now well established in the choicest parts of Palestine under the protection of British guns, these same Jews, having been saved from the fires of Belsen by British sacrifice, showed their gratitude by making sport of their benefactors, as they had done of the Arabs, by getting rid of them in a campaign of such treachery, savagery and indecency, that only the diabolical cunning and carefully prepared directives of THE PLAN could possibly account for it.

Having gained their ends at the expense of the Arabs, the Zionists turned to the next part of their programme—a legal title to Palestine itself, as their own "national home." This they did, with typical cunning, by appealing to world opinion on the grounds of religion—the shop-worn but still effective trick of the Wandering Jew seeking a place of his own to lay his weary head. What better place than his own native land from which he had been "driven" by the Romans when they burned down Jerusalem not long after the Crucifixion? (Actually, the Jews abandoned Palestine when they found that the Romans were standing for none of their nonsense).

Soon their typical campaign of maudlin appeal and bluster had its effect. The usual cranks (of whom this land has more than its fair quota) swarmed to this latest high-sounding cause, just as they were counted on doing. Followed the so-called and mischievous "Balfour Declaration," which in fact, was not at first more than an expression of genteel and pious personal opinion, uttered by Arthur J. Balfour, as a guest at a public dinner.

Unfortunately for us and the peace of the world, the brilliant but somewhat effete Mr. Balfour, darling of that precious mid-Victorian coterie, "The Souls," intellectual and aristocratic forerunners of the more dissolute and unwholesome Bloomsbury aggregation of cranks, crooks and conchies, masquerading as "intellectuals," happened also to be a high ranking member of H.M. Government. As such, what was originally intended to be simply a tactful aside, became news of the utmost political importance. It was instantly seized upon and magnified into an official statement of Government policy by the ever-alert Zionists.

In the hurly-burly of conflicting statements, denials and counter-statements, following upon each other's heels with stunning rapidity, the general public got so tired of the whole controversy and so confused about the issue involved—still another example, you may think, of THE PLAN at work?— that it welcomed the Government's settlement of the whole question. Little did it know then how dearly we and others were to pay for this "settlement," which, in fact, was nothing more than diplomacy's artful way of trying to escape an unwelcome dilemma and make the best of two opposed worlds. For the decision was couched in the following words; obviously intended to protect the Arabs while placating the Jews:

"It being clearly understood that nothing shall be done which may prejudice the civil and religious rights of existing non-Jewish communities in Palestine."

This excerpt was not, of course, the whole of what became known as "The Balfour Declaration." It is chosen here to show how unscrupulous and untrue is the Zionist claim that Britain "promised" them outright and sole possession of Palestine. Incidentally, why we or anyone else should promise them any such thing must remain a mystery to all Gentiles. Could it possibly be, think you, because of their winning ways and engaging habits? Certainly they, with their customary modesty, must think so. For there is no discernible reason in law or justice for their outrageous claim, even in view of the above ambiguous wording. It would therefore appear to be a case of justifying the event afterwards, since conscience doesn't apparently enter into it.

How could practised diplomatists frame a declaration so ambiguous that it was bound to lead to trouble? In any case it was made with "the clear understanding that nothing shall be done which may prejudice the civil and religious rights of existing non-Jewish communities in Palestine." The Jews read into it an absolute unconditional promise by the British Government. Plainly, to anyone who has the least honesty and intelligence the promise was unquestionably *subject to the rights of the Arabs*. The Zionists waged the Palestine war on their interpretation of the Balfour Declaration. The Arabs defended themselves on their interpretation, which appears to most ordinary people as the only honest interpretation. Incidentally they also defended their unquestionable right to Palestine. As Cardinal Hinsley said: "Palestine belongs to the Arabs."

However, these conflicting interpretations of the Balfour Declaration were by no means the underlying cause of the war in Palestine. Something far deeper and more significant lay behind the trouble. Let us see if we can discover, from the historical evidence at hand, just what it was.

In *The History of the Jewish People*, the authors, Margolis and Marx, make the following very significant statement:

"These two things (Jewish nationality and a Jewish State) were taken for granted by the 200 delegates who were all Zionists. It remained to define Zionism and to create the organisation for bringing it into effect. A platform was adopted, the first paragraph of which read Zionism aims at establishing for the Jewish people a publicly and legally assured home in Palestine.' Thus Zionism stepped out into the open..."

Now, whether this is a direct reference to, and report upon, the famous first Zionist Congress at Basle in 1897, is not made plain, but it would appear to be. What is quite certain is that it couldn't be bettered as a proof of the authenticity of THE PLAN and as circumstantial evidence of its designs in view of what did happen in Palestine. Furthermore, it sheds a strong light on why The Zionists rejected not one but several alternative offers made by the British Government in their attempts to find a solution of the Palestine problem that would satisfy both the Arabs, the lawful owners and the Jews, the spurious claimants. For in the same book, (Page 706) we read that Theodore Herzl reported to the sixth Zionist Congress that the British Colonial Secretary offered the Jews a large stretch of land in Uganda for the purpose of nationalising and colonising them under a charter of complete internal economy. The Congress rejected it. Why?

Then there was the famous Argentine scheme launched by Baron Hirsh who bought vast tracts of land in Argentine, as well as in other suitable countries, for Jewish settlement, all to no effect. Only a few Jews took advantage of his generous offer and most of these soon quit and made for the nearest large city. And in time even Herzl became convinced that the Jews wanted Palestine and would accept nothing else, their alleged reason being that it was their spiritual home. So he offered to buy it from the Sultan of Turkey, who curtly declined. Finally, they refused to consider accepting even Madagascar, compared with which the barren and sultry plains of Palestine are a desert.

Therefore, in view of the well-known Jew's avarice and love of getting something for nothing—or at any rate, nothing more than making a nuisance of himself, an exercise that seems to pay dividends as well as give him considerable personal pleasure and satisfaction—it is obvious that they were either fanatically sincere in their claim that they were actuated only by deep love and spiritual attachment to their "native land" or that they had excellent and secret cause to want it badly.

As for the first claim, consider this. They had been "wandering" and settled in every land that could stomach them for over twenty centuries without even once showing this determined and united resolve to claim much less return to Palestine. Why, then, this sudden upsurge of love that was willing to sacrifice all for its ideal? Might not one be justified in thinking it somewhat resembled the story of the missing wife who found her long lost maternal instincts and wifely duty again and returned home as soon as she heard that her husband had inherited a fortune?

As for the second and much more likely reason for Jewry's sudden passion for the land they had abandoned all those centuries ago, consider the nature and extent of the undeveloped wealth of Palestine, probably greater than in any one of the same size throughout the world. The late Lord Moyne, as High Commissioner, openly set his face against a monopoly of this vast undeveloped wealth to any nation or race, so he was assassinated by the Stern gang while The President of "Zionist Federation" boldly, boasted: "The key, to the doors of Palestine is not in the pocket of the High Commissioner but in the pocket of the Jews of New York," and this through the Palestine Corporation of New York! The basis of the struggle in Palestine therefore is obviously a struggle for the monopoly of wealth there and in the Dead Sea area and indicates the answer in stone cold reality.

The following is an extract from the publication "Production of Minerals from the Waters of The Dead Sea Area, 1915"

Potassium Chloride... 2,000 million metric tons.

Magnesium Bromide... 980 million metric tons.

Sodium Chloride... 11,000 million metric tons.

Magnesium Chloride... 22,000 million metric tons.

Calcium Chloride... 6,000 million metric tons.

Potash... inexhaustible.

Carnallite... in excess of Potash.

Oil... estimate not known, but proved to be present by the Standard Oil Company.

Gold... worth approximately £5,000 million (estimate of a French scientist).

These facts were not lost upon Parliament as the following extracts from a speech by Major Legge-Bourke in Parliament, July, 1948, will show:

"As long ago as 1864 it was suggested to the Turks that potash could be produced from the Dead Sea. The date of that is important because it preceded by thirty-three years the first Zionist Congress of 1897. Since then various Zionists have commented on future economic prospects, and, at a meeting addressed by Mr. Ettinger on 29th May, 1929, of the Zionist Federation of Sydney, Australia, Mr. Ettinger is recorded to have said this when referring to the Novomeysky concession which since has become the Palestine Potash Company:

"Had we lost this concession, our whole future in Palestine might have been in danger. All these matters are of an economic nature, but it is this sphere that our political work is most important."

A year before that the Jewish head of I.C.I., Sir Alfred Mond who later became the first Lord Melchett, addressing a conference of Zionists and non-Zionists at the Biltmore Hotel, New York, on 20th October, 1928, said in urging non-Zionist Jews to join the Zionist movement:

"Let me tell you you cannot afford to wait. While we are discussing other people are acting. Whereas we have reports as to the possibilities in Palestine, Gentiles are acquiring land and beginning to take possession of all the best things in the country... If we do not get together and do something within the next five years the opportunity may be so slight, and the ideal we have set before us in Palestine may never be realised. I am not troubling about the economic development of Palestine. That is assured. The problem is, *who will do it*."

The following had a direct bearing on the sordid, explosive quarrel over Palestine. Rufus Isaacs[7] (later Lord Reading and Viceroy of India), conducted an agreement between the British Government and Washington in 1917. It is vital that we should know the details of that

---

[7] Rufus Daniel Isaacs, 1st Marquess of Reading, (1860 – 1935) was a liberal cabinet minister and Viceroy of India. To date, he is the only British Jew to be elevated to a Marquessate. [RB]

agreement because it is believed that important concessions to Jews were given by this agreement. What were they? Knowing this we could possibly learn the beginning of conspiracy which reached its zenith in the embroglio over Palestine:

"The reformed Jew H. H. Klein says that the British Government gave a Zionist Syndicate called 'Palestine Ltd.', all the oil, potash and other minerals of the Dead Sea. This Syndicate was composed of Lord Melchett, Warburg, Guggenheim, Lehman and other Zionist Jews. Mr. Klein values these minerals at 500 billion dollars, and asserts that the invasion of Palestine is for them." (*Traitors*, Armstrong.)

The Patriot of August, 1948, quoted Doctor Homer, M.A. Sc.D., and, coming from one with great personal and scientific knowledge of Palestine, what she says is admonitive, "Long ago I came to the conclusion that financial Jewry—both Zionist and non-Zionist—were furthering the aspirations of fanatical Zionism for its own ends—to gain possession of Palestine... and that it would be kept fallow until such time as they could be developed for the aggrandisement of financial Jewry... financial Jewry has undoubtedly supported the aims of Zionists, moderate, political and economic, because it seeks the political and economic advantages in the struggle for world dominion which Jew-controlled Palestine would afford."

The late Mr. Ernest Bevin, a Foreign Secretary whose untiring labours received the admiration of most people, staked his reputation on settling "the Palestine question" which—as we have seen is no "question." Mr. Bevin was betrayed by "personages behind the scenes," and it is likely that he knew it himself. For instance, settlement was made impossible by President Truman who, with the Jew vote and a General Election in sight, blew negotiations sky-high by demanding the immediate entry of 100,000 Jews into Palestine and at a time when it was difficult enough in all conscience to deal with the situation. It is reported that Truman was warned before the

Presidential Election in November, 1948, that he would lose the Jewish vote if he supported the resolutions submitted to U.N.O. by Great Britain for the calling of sanctions against the Jews if they did not withdraw from Negev[8] in Palestine which had been taken from the Egyptians by the Jews during the truce. A cable was sent from New York to Paris where the delegates were meeting at the time, informing the British delegates that the U.S.A. no longer backed the proposed sanctions to which the U.S.A. agreed. The diplomatic policy of the British Commonwealth had to perform a contortionist act, and became subordinate to the exigencies of the U.S.A. General Election!

Speaking of Communist infiltration into Trades Unions of 15th September, 1948, Mr. Bevin remarked; "We are up against a Plan." Indeed so. Not only in the Trades Unions, but in Palestine and every other country "we are up against a plan" —THE PLAN. As Protocol Nine says;

"The weapons in our hands are limitless ambition, burning greediness, merciless vengeance, hatreds and malice."

And as Protocol seven admonishes;

"In a word, to sum up our system of keeping the governments of the Goyim in Europe in check, we shall show our strength to one of them by terrorist attempts... We must be in a position to respond to every act of opposition by war with the neighbours of that country which dares to oppose us; but if these neighbours should also venture to stand collectively together against us, then we must offer resistance by a universal war."

Mr. Bevin was right. We ARE up against a plan—THE PLAN. The provisions of Protocol 7 and Protocol 9 are rapidly taking shape. At a

---

[8] Count Bernadotte, who was appointed mediator in the Palestine dispute, expressed the opinion that, in all fairness, the Negev should be given to the Arabs. He was assassinated.

Manchester Socialist Conference Mr. Bevin admitted, "It is really, war between Jews and Gentiles." The Jew, Karl Marx said; "Communism can never conquer the world before the British Empire has been overthrown." The age-old plot against Great Britain is made clear by Jew Eberlin in his book. He writes: "the Jews will not get Palestine until the fall of English Imperialism," and the late Sir Stafford Cripps added: "It is fundamental to socialism that the British Empire be liquidated."

There are obviously certain British politicians and public men in league with the Zionists, and their identity is a matter for the electors of Great Britain to demand, if for no other reason than that the Palestine betrayal put a premium on aggression and clamour, as we now know to our cost and shame. As these pages are written Egypt is rattling the sword in the hope that it will persuade Great Britain to scuttle from the Suez Canal, thus cutting our life-line with Australia, New Zealand, India and the Far East. Should any British politician agree to concede to Egyptian demands, his or her identity as a traitor will be clearly exposed.

Before we leave this chapter there is a matter which could well have had a direct influence on the sordid story of Palestine, amounting to betrayal of the nation to Zionist intrigue. The late Chaim Weitzman, first President of the Israeli Government, a Russian-born Jew and ardent Zionist, came to Great Britain early in the century to study chemistry. By the outbreak of war in 1914, he had become a skilful research worker. At a period of serious crisis in the production of munitions Weitzman is said to have discovered an important high explosive. Mr. Lloyd George, then Minister of Munitions, realising the immense value of his discovery, is reported to have asked Weitzman what royalty or reward he would expect for his valuable contribution to the war effort and that Weitzman declined monetary reward, instead asking for an assurance that the British Government would recognise the claim of his race to Palestine on conclusion of the war. When one reflects upon the Balfour Declaration and the secret Anglo-U.S.A. agreement at Washington in 1917 conducted by the late Lord Reading (Rufus Isaacs) it is reasonable to assume that therein resided the ingredients for complying with Weitzman's request for support of the British Government to the outrageous Jewish claim to Palestine.

VI

STATE CONTROL AND THE PLAN

"There is no such thing as eternal justice. Laws are merely the means whereby those in power carry out their will. Human beings have no God-given rights, and therefore are subject to be taken away by man."

STALIN

"The people are governed by very different personages than what is believed by those who are not behind the scenes."

DISRAELI.

THE advocates of so-called State Control offer their panacea as the universal cure for all social, economic and industrial ills that afflict mankind. According to these wishful-thinkers, the moment that "The State" is vested with the control of the essentials of ordinary life, all evils will vanish. At once, everyone will become happy, prosperous, loyal, loving and law-abiding. Moreover, and by some magic formula, the "rights" of even the humblest, most backward and uncouth member of the community, will increase automatically while his duties will decrease proportionately.

The fact that this rosy picture of the millennium, foretold and promised by Socialists, has somewhat faded in the clear light of trial and realism, and that another and much more sinister picture is replacing it every day, is hastily and laboriously explained away by these self-appointed leaders in terms of the aftermath of ancient wrongs, real or fancied; or because of external factors due to the envy and greed of less gifted people; or for other reasons beyond their control. Naturally, nothing is or could be wrong with their ideas—that is, nothing but a few unimportant things like human nature, the immutable laws of supply and demand and the lessons of experience and history. While it is too bad, of course, that such minor considerations should not conform to class-room theories, there is always tomorrow.

Had these delectable products of The London School of Economics been realists or even capable of fundamental thinking, they would have realised that every problem has ultimates as well as superficials and that, in the long run, it is the former that determine the outcome of every scheme, operation and idea. Or, alternatively, had our home-grown Socialists had the gumption to learn from more experienced operators in their own corner of life's laboratory, they would have read and pondered the words by Stalin, quoted above, once the idol of the Bloomsbury coterie, that cancer at the heart of our national way and progress. Not that they would have dared enlighten their followers, already disillusioned enough. For Stalin, master realist, was simply stating the logical outcome of Socialism in whatever Party political disguise it masquerades.

There in a few words is contained the ideology by which regimentation of the individual to successive arbitrary powers is the objective. THE PLAN is based on it, except that the underlying intention is to establish a permanent world order of its own making embodying its own "rights." Yet the Communists claim that "there is no such thing as eternal justice" nor human rights.

This claim that human beings have no inherent rights has no support even in the animal kingdom. It is a conception of human life more bestial than the life of the jungle. But it is a basic principle of THE PLAN. Without it world domination is unattainable.

World domination involves progressive regimentation and frustration of the people in order to serve a specific plan by some self-appointed race of would-be supermen. Certainly no race on earth has been chosen for that purpose.

It is scarcely necessary to draw attention to the increasing intensification of regimentation of the people of this country since the nominal conclusion of World War II. It is all part of THE PLAN. In his book, *The New Despotism*, Lord Chief Justice Hewart, referred to "the flagrant clauses we have had making departments their own Courts; the vast mass of Government by regulation, on top of legislation by order in Council; and 'Department Bills,' the object of which is to shepherd us and regiment us more and more."

It is all being done not, as represented, for the future national welfare, but solely in order to enthrone the State over the individual and make him a mere number on a card index. The people of Great Britain are little more than that already and, unless there is a general uprising against the arrogance of Parliament, regimentation will further increase and freedom become the freedom allowed to caged animals in a zoo.

On all sides is heard complaint against it, but the people have become so apathetic as the result of submitting to regimentation that they seem unable to pull themselves together and impose their will on Parliament.

Excessive State control is not in the interests of a free and happy home life and the development of individuality in accord with Christian tradition, as is strongly realised by "The British Housewives League," for one.

Not so many years ago the people would not have tolerated what they now cravenly submit to, which indicates that THE PLAN for securing world domination, by progressive regimentation of the peoples of each nation in detail, is working out to the satisfaction of our would-be masters.

On every hand bewildered and indignant people are asking the question, "What on earth is happening? Is it possible that these things are happening to us, seven years after the war? What is the meaning of it all" Well, let us see if THE PLAN can enlighten us.

"We have got our hands into the administration of the law, into the conduct of elections, into the press." Protocol 24.

"The Press is entirely in our hands." Protocol 7.

"Literature and journalism are two of the most important educative forces, and therefore our government will become the proprietor of the majority of the journals." Protocol 12.

"Freedom is the right to do that which the law allows... all freedom will be in our hands, since the laws will abolish or create only that which is desirable for us." Protocol 12.

"Useless changes of government to which we instigated the Goyim when we were undermining their State structures will have so wearied the peoples... that they will prefer to suffer anything under us than run the risk of enduring again all the agitations and misery which they have gone through." Protocol 14.

"The best results in government are attained in violence and terrorisation... Protocol 1.

"...Force makes no terms with any right, not even with that of God." Protocol 22.

"Our counter-sign is force and make-believe." Protocol 1.

"Our right lies in force." Protocol 1.

"It will be no disgrace to be a spy and informer, but a merit... in our plan one-third will keep the rest under observation from a sense of duty, on the principle of volunteer service to the State." Protocol 17.

"To us Jews it should be plain to see what a disintegrating importance Communism has upon the minds of the Goyim." Protocol 2.

"The people have raised a howl about the necessity of settling the question of Socialism by way of international agreement. Division into parties has given them into our hands for, in order to carry on a contested struggle one must have money, and the money is all in our hands... in this way the blind force of the people remains our support and we—and we only—shall provide them with a leader and, of course, direct them along the road that leads to our goal." Protocol 9.

"What do we care if the ranks of those striving for power should be thinned, if there should arise a deadlock... a deadlock which will finally disorganise the country?" Protocol 10.

"...Our orators will expound great problems which have turned humanity upside down in order to bring it at the end under our beneficent rule." Protocol 13.

"The daily need for bread forces the Goyim to keep silence and be our humble servants." Protocol 13.

"In order to annihilate the institutions of the Goyim before it is time we have touched them with craft and delicacy, and we have taken hold of the ends of the springs which move their mechanism... we have got our hands into the conduct of Elections." Protocol 9.

"There is nothing more dangerous than personal initiative."[9] Protocol 5.

---

[9] Who to?

"The freedom of the Press, the right of association, freedom of conscience, the ruling principle, and many another that must disappear for ever from memory of man." Protocol 11.

"Our power is in the chronic shortness of food and the physical weakness of the Goyim." Protocol 3.

This means that, no matter what the extent of potential supply for the purpose of implementing The Plan, satisfaction, harmony and contentment cannot be permitted. The necessities of life must be restricted or destroyed, as they have been, to our certain knowledge, for years. For various reasons the people are told that the necessities of life must remain short. Taxation, purchase taxes[10] with other similar illusive devices are used to keep up the "make-believe." How can Christians swallow such blasphemous nonsense? Do Christians believe the truth, that God has afforded man the means for producing plenty for all? It is officially estimated that in Great Britain there are approximately 13,000,000 derelict acres capable of meeting the nation's reasonable requirements with the acreage now under cultivation. Shortages, if they exist, are due entirely to man's own neglect to cultivate the soil in justice and peace. There is no real shortage of the necessities of life. There is an unrealistic shortage, due entirely to the existing financial system which renders it impossible to pay for the means of cultivating, developing and distributing potential plenty.

A certain notorious American Jew propagandist named Vogt wrote a treatise, *Road to Survival*, in which he savagely attacked those who dared to proclaim the truth of plenty for all; and, mark well, plenty for all under a Christian financial system could be obtained without taking anything from anybody, either by taxation or in any other way. Successive governments aid and abet the sacrilegious maxim of

---
[10] To maintain the export racket (vide Chapter 8).

Protocol 3 by the persistent speeches of Members of Parliament about the "necessity for sacrifices". While giving lip-service to Christian principles, Cabinet Ministers, *et alia*, are yes-men to The Hidden Government.

The preface to Vogt's diatribe was written by the world-famous American Zionist financier and "elder statesman," Bernard Baruch, regarded generally as American Jewry's leading banker and unofficial spokesman in all matters of real import. This sacrilegious propaganda is for the purpose of retaining and increasing the control of the people through a financial policy based on the scarcity falsehood. The aftermath of war, with its dislocations, is exploited to the full for keeping up the make-believe. The fact that Baruch wrote the introduction to Vogt's book clearly exposes what the finance tyrants most dread—namely the realisation by Christendom that plenty for all is a plan in God's Creation.

"Government of the people, for the people, by the people" becomes less and less attainable with every move towards greater centralisation of power within the country, and every commitment that reduces the authority of the government over the affairs of its own people without consulting an international or other external arbiter. How long before this process reaches its climax and is reversed by the re-awakened spirit of liberty, self-expression, personal initiative and responsibility in government?" asks the New Zealand journal, *Democracy*.

What does the Hidden Government in its Plan say to this?

"A satisfactory form of government for any country is one that concentrates in the hand of one responsible person" (Protocol 1) —or in Cabinet overlordship (fundamentally the reverse of "government by the people") of which most people are painfully weary.

Obviously, government by the people, in the administrative sense, is an impossibility. "The people" cannot sit in Parliament! The only possible solution lies in democracy of policy and autocracy of method. This entails a very different relationship between the voter and his or her representative from that which exists. If the electorate is not prepared to assume it's right of prerogative of policy it is idle for the people to think they can govern and state control will continue and be intensified. On the other hand, administration (that is, the implementation of policy) is the prerogative of experts. It matters not to the people what methods the experts devise provided they make policy effective and give the demanded results. Here lies the only escape from the strife of party government which is none else than each political party endeavouring in its own way to improve conditions, but always within the framework of a financial system based upon the provisions of The Plan to produce "ferments, disorders and hostility."

Disraeli wrote: "People are governed by words." In reverse it can be translated "people are mis-governed by the misuse of words." Second to none in make-believe is the misuse of the word 'democracy and its misuse in practice. George Wyndham's famous "*Letters*" become the knell of our so-called democratic system and the epitaph of freedom. "Let us quit all the hopeless, helpless dumb show of hypnotised democracy, going to its appointed doom of Bureaucracy and Caesarism, now, everywhere."

VII

THE MONEY-POWER AND THE PLAN

"The final battle for Christianity will be over the money problem, and until that is solved there can be no universal application of Christianity."

BALZAC.

"Give me the power to issue and control the money of a nation and I care not who makes the laws."

A ROTHSCHILD MONEY MASTER OF 100 YEARS AGO.

"All the fields of the machinery of all states go by force of the engine, which is in our hands, and that engine is GOLD!"

PROTOCOL 5.

GOLD is an appropriate substance for making wedding rings and false teeth. As a basis for money it is entirely in-adequate, and is a major cause of economic insecurity, as Protocol 20 foretells.

"The Gold Standard has been the ruin of the states which adopted it, for it has not been able to satisfy the demands for money."

Money is not a commodity, though regarded and operated as such. Money is a mechanism of distribution. If goods and services are available, restriction because of a shortage of money amounts to sacrilege. Goods and services are the correct basis for money. That is a true Christian conception. It is not a Jewish conception and The Plan tells us why:

"We have befooled, bemused and corrupted the Goyim by rearing them in principles and theories which are known to us to be false, although it is by us that they have been inculcated." Protocol 9.

Well may these Frankenstein monsters of our own mistaken indulgence boast as they do in Protocol 22:

"In our hands is the greatest power of the day—GOLD."

Well and truly did Balzac write. The protagonists of The Plan know it.

Let us examine the system popularly referred to as bank-loans or overdrafts.

"By far the larger part of our total money consists of bank deposits." (The late Rt. Hon. R. McKenna, Chairman of the Midland Bank).

Bank deposits consist of two distinct things. Deposits of cash, and deposits created by the banks themselves under the provision of the 1694 Act incorporating the Bank of England. The provision is: "The bank shall have benefit of interest on all money which it creates out of nothing."

How is this done, and how does it affect those who borrow through a bank? How does it affect taxpayers in the case of bank loans to governments? We cannot do better than get the answer from the banks.

"Every bank loan, or overdraft, CREATES a deposit," i.e. creates new money. (McKenna).

"When a bank makes a loan to a customer, or grants an overdraft, in the ordinary course the loan or overdraft will be drawn upon by cheque and paid into someone's credit at the same or another bank. The drawer of the cheque will not have reduced a deposit (already in existence). The receiver of the cheque, when he pays it into his own account, will be credited with its value, and therefore a new deposit (new money) will be created." (McKenna in 1920, when addressing bank share-holders).

It is very important to understand that when a bank makes a loan or grants an overdraft it does not part with anything but ink. It does so by writing the amount required by the customer in figures, backed by a security, on the credit side of his account. Therefore the drawer of a bank-loan or overdraft does not reduce an existing deposit. It can also be seen that new money is created (out of nothing) when the receiver of the cheque pays it into his account.

What it amounts to is this. A bank does not lend its own money, but money, created by it upon a client's security. In other words we pay interest to banks for the privilege of borrowing our own money!

The bank which creates the loan or overdraft "has benefit of interest on all money it creates out of nothing." Obviously, the bank should be paid a final fee for its services, but not annual interest.

"Banks lend by creating credit. They create the means for payment out of nothing." (*Encyclopedia Britannica*, Vol. 15, Money).

"What can I do?" is so often asked. Withhold your vote from any and every candidate who refuses to stand for the reform of this grossly fraudulent system.

"Those who omit the influence of the money power, omit the one thing which renders their judgement worthless." Hilaire Belloc.

VIII

EXPORTS AND THE PLAN

"The economics of usury must be replaced by the economics of what nations can produce."

LORD PORTSMOUTH.

"The primary object of production is consumption."

DOUGLAS.

IN our examination of THE PLAN in relation to the many evils and frustrations that beset us as a people - we who "won the war"! - it may be appropriate to consider here the question of those mysterious things called "exports" which financiers AND politicians of all parties (and none) solemnly warn us are necessary to our survival as a nation. "Export or die!" they cry. And then add, for good measure, "and meantime go without," until we, poor driven oxen, wonder in our dumb, patient fashion, if it is all necessary or just part of some huge plot to keep the blinkers on us while our necks bend to the yoke. Well, let's see.

Having been told that unless we export more than we import we will die, we believe it. (Our rulers are right in one sense, because many of us will die in the inevitable war that such a system makes!) Our rulers do not tell us that some countries enjoying prosperity do so in spite of an adverse balance of trade. The point is how are the exporting countries paid? Before the war Great Britain was probably the largest exporting nation so let us take Great Britain as an example. The question can be put another way; "If the importing nation becomes prosperous on an adverse trade balance how was Great Britain paid when she had a favourable balance of trade?" In fact it means that

Great Britain had a "favourable balance of figures in books." It is a banker's device and works this way.

The exporter obtains a Bill of Exchange on the foreign importer, a document purporting to be an instrument of financial obligation for value received. The Bill of Exchange is presented at an International Discount House and the exporter gets money for it as a bank credit by the process we have already seen in the preceding chapter. This credit the exporter, or the producer, can draw upon to pay wages, etc. The importer meets the Bill of Exchange in due course (i.e. on what is termed maturity) through an International Discount Office, and repayment is banked in the importing country. Actually, what has occurred?

The importer has become possessed of an asset, a piece of paper which authorises him to obtain payment and pay wages, etc, in the same way and by the same process as did the exporter. The books have been balanced. That is all that matters to the financiers. But how about the public? The importer has become possessed of our goods which in very many cases are required by our people. Never mind! The books have been balanced, and the International Discount Offices have pocketed their commissions.

But the story does not end there. Great Britain has suffered inflation because of an increase of money without a corresponding increase in the volume of goods on the home market. On the contrary, goods our people require have been exported. Hence austerity! And here it may be well to note what was written in Protocol Ten:

"These schemes will not turn existing institutions upside down—just yet. They will only effect changes in their economy, and consequently in the whole combined movement of their progress, which will thus be directed along the paths laid down in our schemes."

If any sanity has been left after the insanity of two world slaughter competitions—largely the result of the export-or-die system—the export /import of goods would have been tackled, and the snare of gold been avoided. In a few years of determined effort such as has been put forth by our industrial machine, instead of making goods for export, the Commonwealth, practically self-supporting, could have assumed its rightful position in the exchange with other nations of goods surplus to its own requirements.

Nations do not live by consuming figures in books, Bills of Exchange, nor money in any shape or form. Once nations have produced all they can to satisfy real demand, they can produce for export to supply others with commodities they are unable to produce for themselves. That spells world peace. Whether figures in books are balanced or not what does it matter? If a principle is sound a mechanism can always be devised to implement it.

"We have within the United Kingdom all the primary resources required to provide the essentials of life for our existing population; Britain can live IN THE SENSE OF HAVING ENOUGH FOOD TO EAT, without imports, and therefore without exports." (*From the Ground Up*, Jorian Jenks.) That is to say if we brought the millions of acres of derelict land into cultivation.

But "the personages behind the scenes" have no intention, until forced to by an aroused nation, of forsaking their export/ import plot. This conglomeration of international usurers, as Professor F. Soddy has written, "would sooner see the whole world go up in flames than alter one jot or tittle of their impious self-concocted imperatives."

Which goes a long way to explaining the following passage from Protocol Twenty-two:

"In all that has so far been reported by me to you, I have endeavoured to depict with care the secret of what is coming, of what is past, and of what is going on now, rushing into the flood of the great events coming already in the near future, the secret of our relations to the Goyim of financial operations."

A further factor underlying the Export Drive is hidden from the general public. Politicians, with one or two exceptions, are slaves of the controllers of finance in their determination not to let the people benefit by the modern system of production, i.e. power-driven machinery. The primary objective of all political parties is "Full wage-paid employment," although inventions increase year after year for the special purpose of reducing the possibility of maintaining full wage-paid employment when the aftermath of war has passed. The bonds of economic and political slavery could be broken if it were recognised that abundance with less wage-paid work and more leisure is the important objective underlying technocratic progress.

By the terms of the Bretton Woods Treaty the British Commonwealth markets were opened to America. By the Treaty, America's unemployment problem was exported by her and imported by other countries.

"The agreement is good business. Good business for the industries of America, good business for our farmers and good business for our workers . . . The British (gold) loan agreement is an important step in rebuilding foreign trade and in CREATING JOBS in America." (President Truman, 4th March, 1946.)

As a seller's market fades, as fade it must, and wide-spread unemployment stalks the land, what then? Neither the politicians nor the economic experts attempt an answer. If the people believe that unemployment can be prevented permanently in the modern system of production (except by making work for work's sake—creating jobs) then the people believe "make-believe." The fact is that no one does believe it. Yet, rather than face the facts and re-establish "the established order" to meet modern methods and requirements, laissez-faire is the order of the day in the helpless hope that something will turn up in the darkening future. Something will turn up all right—war and its aftermath; the one and only cure within the framework of "the established order" for securing full wage-paid employment.

"All people " says Protocol Three, "are chained down to heavy toil by poverty more than ever they were chained by slavery and serfdom; from these, one way and another, they might free themselves, these could be settled with; but from want they will never get away?"

The want from which they cannot get away is the want of wage-paid work in this age of technocratic progress. They will certainly not get away from that want while they are ceaselessly drugged into believing that wage-paid work is a moral imperative while labour-saving devices are being increased for the purpose of saving wage-paid labour! "Bled at every vein, this restlessness, which you get everywhere, is the fever of anaemia" is as true to-day and perhaps, even more so, than when Lloyd-George said it after the First World War.

It can now be seen that behind "the export drive" is the urge to force workers to increase production, not for home consumption and utilisation but so that we can balance trade budgets; in the interests not of our people but to bolster up the usurious accountancy of created credits in the sole interest of those who create those credits which are merely figures in books at interest!

In other words; is there a world plot or is there not a world plot? Surely a system which forces the people to work harder than ever before in peace while prohibiting them from consuming and utilising the fruits of their labour is the inversion of simple common sense? Then who benefits by the system? The people? If none benefited, prohibitions and restrictions would cease, as this book contends. So the question remains—WHO BENEFITS?

IX

THE PRESS AND THE PLAN

"The Press, which, with few exceptions that may be disregarded, is already in our hands."

PROTOCOL 7.

"Through the Press we have gained a power to influence while remaining ourselves in the shade."

PROTOCOL 2.

IT is to number 12 of The Protocols that we must turn to get some real idea of the Zionist plot to control the "free" Press of the world in their unceasing campaign for world domination, through fraudulent finance and interlocking cartels that hold, or aim to hold, the world in fee. For there we read the amazing and arrogant words:

"We shall deal with the Press in the following way. What is the part played by the Press? It serves to incite and inflame those passions which are needed for our purpose, or else it serves selfish ends of Parties. It is often vapid, unjust, mendacious, and the majority of the public have not the slightest idea what selfish ends the Press really serves. We shall saddle and bridle it with a tight curb. We shall do the same also with all productions of the printing press, for where would be the sense of getting rid of a tax on the Press if we remained targets for pamphlets and books?"

Again from the same Protocol:

"Literature and journalism are two of the most important educative forces and therefore our Government will become the proprietor of the majority of the Journals."

Thanks to the courage of certain organs of the Press this cocksureness is being gradually dissipated. THE PLAN goes on:

"The Press is entirely in our hands." Protocol 7.

"Not a single announcement will reach the public without our control... if there should be found any who are desirous of writing against us they will not find any person eager to print their productions. Before accepting any production for publication in print the publisher or printer will have to apply for permission to do so."

"Thus we shall know beforehand of all tricks preparing against us and shall nullify them by getting ahead with explanations of the subject treated... This however will in no wise be suspected by the public... The fools who will think they are repeating the opinion of a newspaper of their own camp will be repeating our own opinion and any other opinion that seems desirable for us. In the vain belief that they are following the organ of their Party, they will in fact follow the flag which we hang out for them... By discussing and controverting without touching the essence of the matter, our organs will carry on a sham fight fusillade with the official newspapers... These attacks upon us will also serve another purpose, namely, our subjects will be convinced of the existence of full freedom of speech, and so give our agents an occasion to affirm that all organs which oppose us are empty babblers... Thanks to such methods we shall be in a position to excite or to tranquillise the public mind on political questions, to persuade or to confuse, printing now truth, now lies, facts or their contradictions...We shall have a short triumph over our opponents since THEY WILL NOT HAVE AT THEIR DISPOSITION ORGANS OF THE PRESS IN WHICH THEY CAN GIVE FULL AND FINAL EXPRESSION TO THEIR VIEWS."

No wonder the late and revered G. K. Chesterton wrote:

"Journalism is a false picture of the world thrown upon a lighted screen in a darkened room so that the real world is not seen."

Surely no reasonable person will question Chesterton's authority on his chosen profession? And, as if to underscore his comment, Protocol 12 obligingly says:

"All organs of the Press are bound together by professional secrecy; like the augurs of old, not one of their members will give away the secret of his sources of information unless it be resolved to make announcement of them... So long as they remain the secret of a few the prestige of the journalist attracts the majority of the country—the mob follow after him with enthusiasm. Our calculations are especially extended to the Provinces. It is indispensable for us to enflame there those hopes and impulses with which we could at any moment fall upon the Capital, and we shall represent to the Capitals that these expressions are the independent hopes and impulses of the Provinces. Naturally, the source will be always one and the same—OURS. What we need is that... THE CAPITALS SHOULD FIND THEMSELVES STIFLED BY THE PROVINCIAL OPINION OF THE NATION, i.e. OF A MAJORITY ARRANGED BY OUR AGENTUR. What we need is that at the psychological moment the Capitals should not be in a position to discuss an accomplished fact for the simple reason, if for no other, that it has been accepted by the public opinion of a majority in the Provinces... we must not admit any revelations by the Press of any form of PUBLIC dishonesty... cases of the manifestation of criminality should remain known only to their victims and to chance witnesses—no more."

These extracts from Protocol 12 should be sufficient to convince anyone of the ulterior motive for certain restrictive methods of government and the conspiracy of silence and obstruction by certain organs of public information concerning matters the public should know. These tactics have been copied from Totalitarian States where the safety of rulers and government officials is threatened all the time. Had the Hidden Government not succeeded in persuading successive British Governments to turn Great Britain into a dumping ground for aliens who seek asylum and then proceed to abuse it by spreading the "ferments and disorders" outlined in THE PLAN, this country could be a great deal happier and better place than it is today. And there would be more houses and more food.

The special function of the Press is to convey news and views to the public so that the public may form their own uninfluenced conclusions. Unless the Press is permitted to carry that out, it is not free.

By splitting the Press into a Political Party Press the people are kept divided by warring Party factions. "Divide the people and we will rule," is the unwritten battle-cry underlined in THE PLAN.

X
COMMUNISM AND THE PLAN

"I consider that the immediate suppression of Bolshevism is the greatest issue now before the world, not even excluding the war which is still raging, and unless Bolshevism is nipped in the bud immediately it is bound to spread in one form or another over Europe, and the whole world, as it is organised and worked by Jews, who have no nationality, and whose one object is to destroy for their own ends the existing order of things."

BRITISH GOVERNMENT WHITE PAPER (RUSSIA NO. 1), APRIL, 1919.

"There is no need to exaggerate the part played in the creation of Bolshevism and in the actual bringing about of the Russian Revolution by these international and for the most part atheistical Jews. It is certainly a very great one; it probably outweighs all others. With the notable exception of Lenin, the majority of the leading figures are Jews. Moreover the principal inspiration and driving power comes from the Jewish Leaders."

WINSTON CHURCHILL writing in the *Illustrated Sunday Herald*, 8th February, 1920.

We had been told on many occasions, which we now realise were "timed" for propaganda purposes, that Communism (or, as it was called, Bolshevism) was "not for export." With that soporific, we went happily to sleep; for, in our innocent way, we felt that, so long as Communism was confined to Russia, and they didn't bother us with it, it would do no harm. It was really none of our business. Therefore, we went along quite happily, providing Russia with arms and aid at terrible cost to us when we ourselves needed every gun and penny and man, believing the nonsense that their propagandists both there and here (for the Russian Fifth Column in this country is infinitely more deadly and far-spread than Germany's ever was, in either world war) poured into our willing ears.

What a pity we didn't know then what we know now—that not only is Communism "for export" but that for once the old cry of "Export or die" is true, For, if Communism it not exported to other countries by its secret carriers for transplantation, it will wither and die. For this truth we have no less an authority than Stalin himself. He says in the following words from his book "*Problems of Leninism*" accepted by the "Comrades" and their fellow travellers as their Bible:

"We must proceed... with the development of catastrophic contradictions leading to inevitable wars, with the growth of the revolutionary (i.e. the Socialist-Communist) movement in all countries of the world... Could the Russian Communists confine their work within the narrow national bounds of the Russian Revolution? Of course not. On the contrary, the whole situation impelled them to transfer the struggle to the international arena."

The Zionists are war-makers. Their purposes are international communism and a world super-government. The simple remedy to avoid war is to get rid of the Zionists and their satellites from government, and all key positions.

Years have passed since Germany and Japan surrendered. The Communists have taken advantage of this desired delay, to starve and intimidate the people of Europe and force them to embrace Communism. They have taken advantage of the veto provision of the Charter to veto everything that is designed in any way to help the distressed of Europe or check the march of Communism. In the meantime the Communists are conquering the people and nations of

Europe, and, through the labour organisations, they are making war upon us here at home. Which is exactly as forecast in Protocol 5:

"By all means we shall so wear down the Goyim that they will be compelled to offer us INTERNATIONAL POWER of a nature that by its position will enable us without violence gradually to absorb all the State forces of the world and to form a Super-government. In place of the rulers of today we shall set up a bogey which will be called the Super-government Administration. Its hands will reach out in all directions like nippers and its dimensions will be of such colossal dimensions that it cannot fail to subdue all the nations of the world."

Now the question must be faced, because it is so often asked and discussed among all classes of people who could no more be accused rightly, of "Jew-baiting" than they could be of bear-baiting, Are the Russian Communists Jews?" Before attempting to answer that important question let us re-word it. First let us substitute the word "Jewish" and then put the question like this: "Is Russian Communism Jewish?" Because, obviously, whatever the founders and present leaders of Communism in Russia may be, there are millions of Communist adherents, willing and unwilling, who are not Jews. That applies to Communists all over the world. Therefore, let us be quite fair about this, and not make a sweeping statement that is not only absurd but is also, by implication, unjust.

That Communism was originated by Jews (Marx and Trotzky being the best known) cannot be disputed if only for the reason that these men never tired of proclaiming their achievement, once it was safe to do so. Nor were their co-religionists slow to claim the sole credit for Jewry when Communism was socially "fashionable." Therefore, in discussing a question of the utmost public importance we are not only well within our rights, but it becomes imperative to find out all we can about its leaders, the better to understand and weigh the question before us. Let no man, therefore, raise the cry of "Jew-baiting" or "witch-hunting," lest he stand condemned as one who fears the light of investigation, preferring to lurk in the shadows of doubt.

The famous English historian, Hilaire Belloc[11], says on this question: "As for anyone who does not know that the Bolshevist movement in Russia is Jewish, I can only say that he must be a man who is taken in by the suppressions of our deplorable Press," while A. N. Field [12]writes in *To-day's Greatest Problem*: "Once the Jewishness of Bolshevism is understood, its otherwise puzzling features become understandable. Hatred of Christianity, for instance, is not a Russian characteristic; it is a Jewish one."

Thus it is not the Russian people who threaten world peace, but the cold, calculating Judaic-Communists who seized power after their 1917 Revolution, with their pious make-believe of "freeing the peoples " whose sufferings to-day arc far greater than they ever were under the Czarist regime, according to Victor Kravchenko (who fled from the "Red Terror") in his book; *I Chose Freedom*.

There are indisputable facts to prove that Communism is Jewish. The Jews who surrounded Stalin and now Malenkov include the brothers Kaganovitch, Varga and Asberg. There is Manuilsky over Ukraine, until recently Anna Pauker and now Gheorghiu-Dej in the 'Rumanian' Government, Rakosi in Hungary, Amsterdamski in Poland - all Jews. In all these Governments, not the odd Jew here and there, but hosts of Jews hold the majority of the key posts. According to *The Times* of 19th April, 1949, the Jew Moshe Pijade has "great influence" in

---

[11] Hilaire Belloc (1870 – 1953) was an Anglo-French writer and historian. He was one of the most prolific writers in England during the early twentieth century. He is most notable for his Catholic faith which had a major impact on his writing and for his association with G.K. Chesterton. He was also a Member of Parliament. [RB]

[12] Arthur Nelson Field (1882 –1963) was a New Zealand right wing journalist, author and theoretician. [RB]

Yugo-Slavia. It is the same everywhere behind the Iron Curtain. It is the same this side of the Iron Curtain. It was the same among the Communists who attempted to seize Spain and called the recent Dock Strike in Britain, and who are at the bottom of unofficial strikes with which progress is plagued. And what could there be but a Jewish motive for the present persecution of the Christian Church?

Yet, while their most spectacular successes are to be seen in Russia, it is right here in Great Britain that they have gained their greatest potential from the point of view of The Zionists and therefore THE PLAN. Let there be no mistake about that. For while Communism, the sword of Israel, has reddened the plains of Eastern Europe and is swinging in ever-widening circles over the vast fields of Asia, it is broken unless it can conquer Great Britain. That fact is recognised by "The Fourteen Men in the Kremlin." It is for that reason that we contend that the Zionists have accomplished their most important success by their policy of infiltration into the key positions of public life here.

Already we have experienced the paralysing hand of delay and frustration in our foreign affairs, worth many military divisions to Communism in its relentless warfare upon our way of life, and therefore upon our very lives and freedom. The cruder forms of national sabotage, thinly disguised as "unofficial strikes" engineered by thugs and malcontents, for the most part, string-pulling their bemused puppets; the shabby and often ridiculous demonstrations, meetings and "petitions" —which, by the way, are, as any advertising man knows, merely devices to compile what are contemptuously called in the trade, "sucker lists for the high-pressure boys to work on at their leisure for the purpose of getting new members and, more important, more revenue for the Party—and even the beggarly and bedraggled "Party" itself, with its high-falutin nonsense, solemn airs and crude propaganda, can rightly be left safely to the police to watch. But infiltration into high office is quite another matter. On this point, we could not do better than consider what Hilaire Belloc has to say in his book, *The Jews*:

"The Jew pointed to the English State as that one in which all that his nation required of the Goyim was to be found. He here enjoyed a situation the like of which he could not hope to enjoy in any other country in the world. All antagonism to him had died down. He was admitted to every institution in the State. A prominent member of his nation became chief officer of the English Executive. With an influence more subtle and penetrating, marriages began to take place wholesale, between what had once been the aristocratic territorial families of this country and the Jewish commercial fortunes—English families in which there was no Jewish blood were the exception... Every English government had (and has) its quota of Jews. They had entered the diplomatic service and the House of Lords; they swarmed in the House of Commons and in the Universities... They were all-powerful in the Press; they were all-powerful in the City."

According to Hyamson's *History of the Jews*, all this has been brought about in little more than a hundred years. For, "there were only 30,000 Jews in the British Isles as late as 1830, and they were not allowed any of the privileges of citizenship; they could not vote, hold office, practice law or medicine, or teach in the schools.[13] Now they virtually own and operate the British Empire. Such is the power of those in control of the Press, banks and financial houses, here, there, everywhere."

According to Disraeli, in *Coningsby*, when he, a baptised Jew, was Prime Minister, the Jew was the power behind the throne in every European country. Such was the persistence and ubiquity of the Jew not only here but everywhere, For, though 1897 was the date of laying down the programme for world domination, political activity began soon after 1792, during the French Revolution which Jewry claims to

---

[13] And this is what should be done again.

have engineered and which, in its excesses, they certainly dominated, according to Voltaire; until it had made such progress that Baron Lionel Rothschild became an M.P.

As for the political influence of the millions of Jews in the U.S.A. it is such that they were able to dictate the complete betrayal of the Palestine Agreement by the White House, as the price of Truman's re-election in 1948. By their clamour and hysterics, coldly directed by their Zionist leaders; by their large scale exploitation of latent racial feeling at the expense of the British—they who so bitterly wail about "Racial prejudice"!— through mass advertising in the Press; by other and more hidden means, they are in practical control of the political destiny of the U.S.A., and through her, of the Western World. The other half, their blood brothers in the Kremlin already and literally control.

All of which runs true to plan. Writing in 1927, Reni Gross, a French Jew, said, in *Nouveau Mercure*: "The two internationales of Finance and Revolution work with ardour. They are THE TWO FRONTS of the Jewish Internationale... There is a Jewish conspiracy against all nations."

What does all this mean? That the conquest of Britain is from within and that this fortress of freedom is being betrayed more by her indifference to danger and by her mistaken tolerance of the enemies within her gates, than by poltroons and traitors like Nunn-May and Fuchs, evil as they are, and far-reaching as their betrayals may prove. If there be still any doubt in any mind about this, let him ponder the whitewashing of these traitors by the "Left-wing" journalists of Fleet Street, ever eager to tilt at the windmills of their neurotic dislikes, while blind to the giant of destruction at their backs.

Meanwhile, let these apologists for such traitors rejoice to think that Fuchs, for one, has found time and been given facilities, while in prison, to write a book, *I Found Peace*. Let us hope that his peace won't be unduly disturbed by the visions of the multitudes, including many British service-men that his betrayal sent to hideous death. For they too found peace, THE PEACE OF DEATH.

XI

CHRISTIANITY AND THE PLAN

"Christianity will be abolished."

THE above astonishing words occur in the following passage from a published speech, delivered in August, 1949, by M. A. Levy, Secretary, "World League of Liberal Jews," Los Angeles, California.

"To-day the Gentile Christians who claim of holy right have been led in the wrong path. We, of the Jewish Faith have tried for centuries to teach the Gentiles a Christ never existed, and that the story of The Virgin and of Christ is, and always has been, a fictitious lie. In the near future, WHEN THE JEWISH PEOPLE TAKE OVER THE RULE OF THE UNITED STATES, legally under God Jehovah, we will create a new education system, proving that Jehovah is the only one to follow, and proving that Christ story a fake... Christianity will be abolished."

Lest Levy's outburst be dismissed as the isolated ravings of a Jewish monomaniac, instead of considered seriously as indicative of a world-wide plot for the overthrow of Christianity and of all it stands for in the hearts and lives of men, consider this further declaration by Rabbi Benamozegh:

"Zionism can be considered as a touchstone... The Jew is not satisfied with de-Christianising, he Judaises: he destroys the Catholic or Protestant Faith, he provokes indifference, but he imposes his idea of the world, of morals and of life upon those whose faith he ruins: he works at his age-old task, the annihilation of the religion of Christ."

While dismissing the language in which the above quotations are phrased as typical Jewish extravagance, and ignoring the arrogance of the assumption in both declarations, intended originally for exclusive

Jewish consumption and inspiration, particularly Levy's insolent reference to the Government of the USA., it is reasonable to assume that they stem from a common root. This assumption is emphasized by the quotations below from The Protocols themselves, to which all Zionists turn for inspiration and unquestioned guidance:

"We have long past taken care to discredit the Priesthood of the Goyim, and thereby ruin their mission on earth which might be a hindrance to us. Day by day its influence on the peoples of the world is falling lower. Freedom of conscience has been declared everywhere, so now only years divide us from the moment of the complete wrecking of the Christian religion..."

Again:

"The King of the Jews will be the real Pope of the universe, the patriarch of the international church... we shall fight against them (the churches) by criticism calculated to produce schism."

These directives for the Sons of Levi occur in Protocol 17. To show that they have not gone unheeded by the faithful, here are a few more extracts from the writings and sayings of individual members of the restless tribe. First, as is befitting, we'll quote the Chief Architect of the Zionist world conquest and moulder of the teachings of Hegel into the technique of the Communist crusade. Hear, then, Karl Marx himself on Zionism versus Christianity:

"The Jews have emancipated themselves in their own fashion in that Christians have become Jews."

The unusual mildness of the fiery Marx's words strike a pleasing contrast to those of his followers whose venomous declarations are listed below, with the identity of their proud authors bracketed alongside:

"I spit on your religion. The law of God does not exist in Soviet territory." (Jew Kylenko, Soviet Commissar for Justice.)

"The anti-religious campaign of the Soviet must not be restricted to Russia. It must be carried on throughout the world." (Jew Stephanov.)

"We hate Christianity and Christians. Even the best of them must be regarded as our worst enemies. They preach love of one's neighbour and mercy, which is contrary to our principles. Christianity is an obstacle to the development of the revolution. Down with love of one's neighbour! What we need is hatred. We must know how to hate, only thus shall we conquer the universe." (Lunacharsky, Soviet Commissar of Education.)

"With all my heart I wish Bezbojnik every success in its warfare against the revolting spectre of God." (Lunacharsky.)

For good measure, let us now examine the gentle words of another Jew on the subject of Christianity; this time one who, because of his work for the stage and films, is more than merely an unknown name in brackets after a quotation, We now quote from the notorious animadversion of that true lover of all mankind, Ben Hecht, self-appointed scourge of the hated Christians and darling of his entrenched tribe everywhere. We quote, of course, from his book, *A Jew in Love:*

 "One of the finest things ever done by the mob was the crucifixion of Christ. Intellectually it was a splendid gesture. But trust the mob to bungle. If I'd had charge of executing Christ I'd have handled it differently. You see, what I'd have done was had him shipped to Rome and fed him to the lions. They never could have made a Saviour out of mincemeat."

It is tempting to dismiss this outburst by Hecht as the ravings of a diseased mind, until one remembers that it was part of a cold-blooded campaign being waged by American Zionists and their credulous dupes against Great Britain; and that Hecht's book actually carried an appendix calling for a boycott by Americans of all British goods. One must conclude, therefore, that it represents Hecht's measured contribution to the overthrow of something he has been taught to hate from his earliest days in the stews of Chicago's stock yards, from which, it would appear he has never emerged emotionally. That something is Christianity, whose staunchest champion is still Great Britain. Hence this fanatical tirade in all its revolting vulgarity and offensiveness. Incidentally, it sows the seeds of its own destruction, because the dragon's teeth it grows form the block houses of yet another Belsen. And, for Hecht's sake, let us hope that there may be again on hand the might of Christian Britain to rescue him and his like from its consuming furnaces.

Nevertheless, it would be a betrayal of everything we stand for as a Christian people were we to ignore the implications of the foregoing quotations—the implacable hatred of Christianity, as Christianity, and the wide-spread, utterly ruthless Zionist campaign to overthrow it. It is our duty and privilege to stand up for our principles, our beliefs and our faith and to defend them against the enemies of Christ, as our fathers did before us. Nor can we plead that we did not know the danger, or our duty. For, in their boastfulness, The Zionists have made their opinion of both Christians and Christianity quite clear.

Perhaps the following quotation from the Gospel according to St. John gives a clue to just why Zionism is so virulent in its hatred of the gentle Nazarene who said to the Jews: "Ye are from beneath... ye are of this world." (Translated into other words, "You are materialists, I am not.") And again: "Ye seek to kill me.. If God were your Father, ye would love me... ye are of your father the devil." (John VIII). (Note that in the Bible "Father" is spelt with a capital when referring to the Christian God, and with a small "f" when referring to Jehovah the tribal god of the Jews.)

If this passage from The New Testament is taken in conjunction with the following excerpt from Protocol 14 based on The Old Testament, the true meaning of the underlying conflict between Judaism and Christianity begins to be clear:

"When we come into our kingdom it will be undesirable for us that there should exist any other religion than ours... we must therefore sweep away all other forms of belief. If this gives birth to the atheists it will not, being only a transitional stage, interfere with our views."

The pillars of the Christian Church are founded on a rock; dynamite has been and is still being laid secretly beneath them. Consider the Treaty of The Lateran, sometimes referred to as the Lateran Pact. On June 7th, 1929, Cardinal Gasparri received from Mussolini a note of the Bank of Italy for 750 million lire, accompanied by conditions.

Probably most vital to The Roman Catholic Church was Article 20 of the Treaty by which Bishops, before taking up their diocese, had to take an oath of fidelity to the Fascist State—no Bishop being appointed if the Government vetoed his appointment.

For the loss of Vatican territory—the Papal States—the Pope received 16 million lire, partly cash and partly Italian bonds.

Would these huge sums have been paid to the Vatican unconditionally? Many Roman Catholics who know the terms of the Treaty express disgust at what, on the face of it, looked like the defacement of spiritual values for material gain—a surrender to sordid materialism. In Mussolini's own words; "These accords are a political and financial convention with a Fascist imperative."

By the Treaty the education of youth was transferred entirely to the Fascist State, a circumstance alluded to in an article in *The Listener* by George Martelli as "the Pope becoming the prisoner of Mussolini."

It was just another step in accordance with THE PLAN for "discrediting the priesthood of the Goyim." By coming under the heel of the Italian Government on the Government's own terms the Roman Catholic Church surrendered the substance of its universal character. A mess of pottage had done its deadly work.

The Church of England is strangled with its tribute to usury. Few churches are not in debt to the banks by loan or overdraft. The whole Christian Church is in the clutches of "the synagogue of Satan." Unaware of this, many devout Christians would indignantly deny it.

Consider Socialism, Communism, Bolshevism; outward expressions of THE PLAN'S tactic to "wreck the Christian religion." Communism derives from Socialism, and Socialism derives from orthodox financial policy constituting an outrage on Christian ethics. Says Gaudin in *The Dreary Dilemma*, "Just as the Conservative fails to grasp the finance of which he approves, generally without understanding, produces Socialism, so the Socialist fails to grasp in his turn that their end product, Communism, is derived from persistence in orthodox finance. The people who control finance are well aware of this, but as their aim is centralised power they use any means that will serve their ends. Control is now both through money and 'planning.' The first, hidden to most as to its working, has an admirable means of control as the sufferers have not realised what has hit them. To-day by the introduction of bureaucratic methods and Statutory Instruments the policy of the controllers comes into the open..."

Before rejecting these revelations and enquiries as "bigoted," let all Christians ponder the following ten commandments of the Communist Youth. They were issued by *The Bolshevik*, a Russian monthly magazine, December, 1946.

I. Never forget that the Priests are the bitterest enemies of the Communist State.

II. Persuade your friends towards Communism. Stalin is the head of the Godless throughout the world.

III. Advise your friends and the Godless to steer clear of the Priests.

IV. Beware of spies, and bring to light those engaged in sabotage (of Communism).

V. Disseminate atheistic literature among the population.

VI. A real member of the Komsomol is, at the same time, a militant atheist.

VII. Wherever possible wage war against the religious elements and prevent their influence.

VIII. A real godless must be an efficient policeman. It is the duty of every atheist to protect the safety of the State. Just as our brethren are obliged, at their own risk, to denounce to the Kabal apostates of their own family, or members who have been noticed doing anything in opposition to the Kabal[14], so in our kingdom over all the world it will be obligatory for all our subjects to observe the duty of service to the State in this direction . . . So placed as to have the opportunity in their disintegrating activity of developing and displaying their evil inclinations, obstinate self-conceit, irresponsible exercise of authority, and, first, and foremost, "venality."[15]

IX. Support the godless movement with financial contributions which are particularly needed for foreign propaganda.

X. You cannot be a good Communist without being a convinced atheist.

---

[14] The Kabal is the secret science of the Jewish Rabbi for their interpretation of Scripture said to be handed down by oral tradition. The 1897 Zionist Conference was for instance, a Kabalistic Conference.

[15] Protocol 17. "It will be no disgrace to be a spy and informer, but a merit."

And, as if that were not enough, Protocol 14 boasts that THE PLAN provides for the further corruption of youth as follows:

"In countries known as progressive and enlightened we have created a senseless, filthy, abominable literature."

If our Christian clergy, dedicated to the service of their Master, would conclude their mission on earth, they must save the Christian Church from itself. Judaism has hypnotised the Priesthood. "Ye cannot serve God and mammon" still holds true. Neither can the Priesthood serve God and Judaism; Christian doctrine and Judaic doctrine; nor encourage their flocks to do so and expect to fill their churches.

Their motive when they champion Zionism may be Christianly, but they might just as well erect stained glass windows to Satan over their altars. What is the Alleluia Chorus but a paean of praise to the Judaic god! The word "Alleluia" means "All praise to Jehovah."

Why do church leaders complain of empty churches? Is it not because they are discredited? What do they offer? The tenets of the Sermon on the Mount WITH SIGNS FOLLOWING by the raising of the sick, the sinning and the dead?

Sin, disease and death are only degrees of evil. Sin being the easiest to combat, the Church concentrates on sin; but the overcoming of the other degrees of evil should be included in the mission of the Priesthood. If the Priesthood understood their mission as vicars of Christ with signs following, their churches would be filled to overflowing with willing disciples.

The people would seem to be more progressively minded than their pastors. They are tired of "Lord! Lord!" and faith without works, tired of asking for bread and being given a stone, tired of just church-going with organ recitals and incantations, ornate churches, priests in more or less ornate vestments, altar cloths covered with Kabbalistic symbols, set prayers and vain repetitions to a dualistic god ground out weekly as on a prayer-wheel in which the Omniscience is told what to do, and collective and individual "absolution" given by men little or no better than their flock.

So long as Christian service consists of blind faith without works, so long will the Priesthood fail in their labour. Was not the hallmark of a Christian clearly defined? "He that believeth on me the works that I do shall he do also." What answer has the Priesthood to that? Claiming to be His vicars, the Priesthood should know. But do they? The promise was unmistakable. It stands as a daily challenge to all who profess His name and invoke His power. If they do not understand their claim is false.

A Minister of the Church of Scotland and Hebrew scholar informed the author that the word "believe" as used in the English language differs from the Hebrew meaning which is "understanding." When, therefore, Our Lord said; "He that believeth on me..." he meant "He that understands my teaching with its practical application to the ills of humanity, the works that I do shall he do also." To believe is one thing; to understand His teaching is the test. It is this practical understanding with signs following the people look for from the Priesthood. The Priesthood excuse themselves by claiming that the works He did were supernatural. On the contrary, they were the test and natural result of understanding, of knowing.

The smugness of the Priesthood is nauseating. "By their fruits ye shall know them." What are their fruits? Untiring devotion to their calling and often self-sacrificing labour to comfort and help others; but these things are not the only fruits expected of them. Articles appeared in the daily press during August, 1948, drawing attention to the "apathy threat to the Churches." One of these articles reads:

"Dr. Wand, Bishop of London, to-day told the assembly of the Council of Churches that they had to counter a growing 'what-the-hell attitude?' among the masses of people in countries like Great Britain and the United States. The existing challenge is a challenge to the Church."

Even so. A challenge to the Church and the Christianity taught, not a challenge to the people. Pastor Niemoller, German Protestant Leader, warned the Church not to awaken false hopes, he said;

"It is beyond our power to restore order to this chaotic world." This from men who have constituted themselves teachers of Christian doctrine. The people cannot accept judgement from those who are judged. How can the people follow leaders who openly admit they are powerless? Can the people be blamed for their "what-the-hell" attitude? Instead of blaming the people for apathy and chaos let the Priesthood remember the admonition "Judge not that ye be not judged."

The poison of State tyranny pervades the world, yet the Christian Church remains almost silent in the face of this satanic onslaught. The pagan path of Satanism has wormed its way through all Christian countries, and the Priesthood and politicians go about their daily activities, seemingly unaware of the real purpose behind total planning and unlimited central power. There is no place for freedom from fear in a society constituted as a soulless power-driven machine. The Planned submit to it all because of the "make-believe" that they receive monetary benefits, which benefits they themselves subscribe to through taxation! State tyranny (unlimited central power) means the removal of the moral landmarks which imposes limitation on the exercise of human initiative. The deprivation of the individual of personal initiative means surrender to a hidden power acting through government; and if Christians are to survive effectively they must mobilise in their millions against the insidious doctrines of the pagan empire in their midst, which for years has been mobilising to defeat them.

There are signs that the Church may be waking up to its culpable neglect, though at present comparable to a weak voice crying in the wilderness of human vexations. On Sunday, 29th August, 1948, Dr. Hutchinson-Cockburn of the Church of Scotland, appealed to the whole Council of Christian Churches to meet the inroads of the State on human rights. Dr. Cockburn said; "This most dangerous colossus of the day will reduce mankind to servile obedience. It will rob him of his rights and privileges."

Will? If the Priesthood would only condescend to consider the nature of the path of the snake, how it has long since wormed its way into the Church while the Priesthood decries THE PLAN as a forgery, they would know exactly how to proceed in their effort; to save the Church. Led by the Priesthood it would involve the clash of People versus Parliament. If the Church leaders are not courageous enough to take their stand and give the lead they may as well forsake all idea of Christian revival.

The following propositions are essential to Christian philosophy.

1. That it is essential that the Group shall have no conscriptive power over the individual; i.e., the individual must have the power to contract out of any group.

2. That maximum decentralisation of initiative is in the interest of human welfare.

Christians exhibit little earnestness in defence of their full birthright and estate. Consider the earnestness with which the Satanism of Communism goes to work. "The attitude of a political party towards its own mistakes is one of the most important and surest ways of judging how earnest the party is... Frankly admitting the mistake, ascertaining the reason for it, analysing the conditions which led to it, and thoroughly discussing the means of correcting it. That is the earmark of a serious party."—*Selected Works*—Lenin. Such is the method of Communism. Such should be the method of Christians if they would combat their greatest enemy effectively. They have many mistakes to admit, and the first to admit is their divided allegiance between Christianity and Judaism, between the practical Christianity of its Founder and the satanic materialism of Judaism. There can be no compromise. Christians must not be anti-Jew. They must be anti-Judaism in a Christian International with chastened Canterbury, and Rome the guiding star.

The Church Assembly, 1948, condemned Marxist-Communism. Why does the Church Assembly not condemn Judaism, Marxist-Communism in disguise, "fundamentally anti-Christian"? The so-called Jewish problem is not THE problem. **The problem is the Christian problem.** It is not the prerogative of Christians to look for a solution of the Jewish problem, but for a solution of their own problem.

General Ludendorf, the famous German strategist, who admired the British, wrote in 1931 in his book, *The Coming War*: "The majority of the English do not realise that, having done their duty by the inner Jewish circle, they have now to disappear as a world power." Ludendorf's statement contains an interpretation which was certainly not in his mind. It might be interpreted, "The majority of the Priesthood do not realise that having done their duty by the inner Jewish circle, the Christian Church has now to disappear."

Having succumbed to Judaic influences, its Priesthood discredited as foretold in THE PLAN, the Church is not blameless for the declension and chaos we now see going on before our eyes. The Jew understands perfectly what he is about. The Christian is mentally myopic to it all. The Jew has got the Christian where he wants him, and the Christian is too much a gentleman to believe that such an immoral, satanic plan could be in existence, far less affect him.

The fact remains that the shape of things as they are, in which Christian is decimating Christian morally, physically, politically and economically, is proof that something IS affecting the Christians and their Church. What that "something" is, is set forth clearly in the First Protocol; and the others quoted below:

"If it is allowed and not considered immoral to use every manner and art of conflict, as for example to keep the enemy in ignorance of plans of attack and defence... then in what way can the same means in regard to a worse foe (Christianity)... be called immoral?"

"Let us, however, in our plans direct our attention not so much to what is good and moral as to what is necessary and useful." Protocol 1.

"The people do not lay a finger on him who hypnotises them by his daring and strength." Protocol 15.

"If we give the nations a breathing space the moment we long for is hardly likely ever to arrive." Protocol 10.

"It was said by the prophets that we were chosen by God Himself to rule over the whole earth. God has endowed us with genius that we may, be equal to our task." Protocol 5.

Read in conjunction with the shape of things as they are, the Zionist claim above that God Himself has approved their stratagem should scarcely commend itself to the Christian Church.

How can the Church expect to accomplish her task on earth if THE PLAN is dismissed lightly as a forgery? Recognition of the mental undermining process going on incessantly behind the scenes should bring the Church to grips with the false proposition, laid down in THE PLAN, that the whole conception of "good" and "moral" is a fallacy.

Prayers for the success of the United Nations General Assembly held in September, 1948, were offered by the Hierarchy of the Christian

Church. They expressed the hope that the United Nations[16] "might save the world." They drew attention to the maelstrom of violence, convulsions and discontents in which millions are caught. Everyone hopes for peace and plenty. The plenty is available, and only the Judaic financial system which is part of THE PLAN, is purposely preventing its distribution.

In this latter connection, The Christian Social Council of England (circa 1923) has made this forthright and urgent demand; "That the Christian Church should recognise frankly, and clearly expose such results of the present monetary system as appear harmful to human welfare; and should further declare that any monetary system must have objectives in accord with Christian ethics." And this is 1954!

Frankly, what should be the objective? To introduce a monetary system which BENEFITS ALL AND PENALISES NONE, the integral function and sole purpose of money. The only response to that demand has been to intensify socialistic finance which benefits selected minorities while penalising the nation.

Even now, after World War II, there is plenty for all. "At last we have it, and it is something we have long suspected. The British ration is regulated not so much by a food shortage as by a financial policy." (Editorial, *The Daily Mail*, 10th July, 1946.) The same with many other things. Subtle imperatives working on the mind of the peoples in all nations are "turning every form of government into OUR despotism." (Protocol 10.) As witness:

"It is indispensable to trouble in all countries the peoples' relations with their governments so as to utterly exhaust humanity with dissension, hatred, struggle, envy, and even by the use of torture and starvation, that they find refuge in our complete sovereignty in money..." Protocol 16.

---

[16] A Jew ridden organisation.

Compare this devilry with what is going on here, there and everywhere, all paving the way to Communism and world domination; the peoples having become so utterly exhausted that they may "take refuge" in any form of government, their former governments having become entirely discredited.

That is the unmistakable challenge that faces Christianity to-day. Christianity is on trial for its life, and unless it awakens to that fact before it is too late, and takes immediate and adequate measures to meet the challenge, it is doomed.

Its adversary is Zionism—not some mythical and long-dead figure of evil, but a living, breathing, alert and cruel organisation, working to and through a plan—THE PLAN—that has one object, the complete overthrow of Christianity and the subjection of mankind to the worship and service of its tribal god, Jehovah.

Before the Divine Mission, Jewry had had it all its own way. He exposed the sin of Jehovistic doctrine and worship. This aroused Jewry's venomous hostility, ending in the trumped-up charge on which he was tried; and, because of public clamour for his death, though unconvicted he was crucified. By killing the Man Jesus, the Jews thought to kill the Christ, the truth concerning God and man. They soon found that the crucifixion had failed in its intention. The Plan, though discovered in the 19th century, is nothing new. It reveals the age-old stratagem by which Jewry hopes to complete the destruction of Christianity by the perversion of Christian values.

The choice for the Christian Church, as well as for everyone who calls himself a Christian is God or Jehovah, and depending upon that choice will be the fate of the world.

Once more the ancient cry goes up - "Whom choose ye?" And this time there can be no washing of hands.

XII

IS THIS THE ANTI-CHRIST?

"Now only years divide us from the moment of the complete wrecking of the Christian religion."

PROTOCOL 17.

"Christianity is writhing in its last throes of death, and the World's favourite idol is fading into obscurity."

UNITED ISRAEL BULLETIN OF NEW YORK, U.S.A., JUNE, 1951.

THE great difficulty that most Christians will have in reading this book will be to reconcile what has been disclosed in the preceding chapters with what they have been taught about God. For to them, the word God is interchangeable with Jehovah, whereas, as these pages clearly show, that is not so. Let us get this very important point straight, because, until we do, we shall be bogged in doubt.

First of all, Jehovah, was the name the Israelites gave to their conception of God; and, for many years, even the tribes of Israel were divided on this question, as they were about most others. Thus we learn that Jehovah was, at first and for a long time, the name that only one tribe gave to God, and that tribe was the tribe of Levi. Nor is it likely that it would ever have been adopted by the other tribes, had not Moses been a Levite. From which it can safely, be deduced that the name Jehovah would have remained entirely a tribal matter but for that circumstance.

Incidentally, there was nothing unanimous about either the spelling or the meaning of the word when it was adopted by the twelve small, nomadic and pillaging tribes that made up the Jewish race. Indeed, both spelling and meaning varied so widely that it is doubtful if any one tribe agreed with any of the others about what or who Jehovah was. Nor was it a matter of concern to most of them. The general idea in adopting the name Jehovah was to pay a personal compliment to Moses for his overall leadership. Therefore, any idea that Jehovah was always the God of the Jews can be dismissed at once.

Second, the Jewish concept of Jehovah was, and still is, quite different from the Christian concept of God. Jehovah to the Jews was a war-like God; a God of vengeance, swift to anger and to punish. Christians defined God simply and fully as God of Love.

Third, the aggregation of Jewish tribal histories, legends and literature that go to make up what Christendom came to regard as "The Old Testament" were so saturated with stories of slaughter, rape, plunder, revenge, hate and horror, that no sane person could regard the Jehovah of Israel with anything but repugnance.

There we have the whole explanation of the Crucifixion and the unceasing warfare upon Christianity by Zionism ever since. He came to expose and end their evil teaching, to drive them from the Temple they profaned. In his own words, "I came not to send peace but a sword." For that they never forgave him, and until they can crucify him again—this time on their cross of gold—they will never rest content.

Fourth, so long as the Church of Christ confuses God and Jehovah, the world must continue to be divided and at war, one with the other, and the fundamental truth of the brotherhood of man remain obscure and merely a pious hope. For figs are still not gathered from thistles; which means that only by discarding the "Old Testament" (except as literature and legend) as a source of inspiration and authority, can the pure Gospel of Christianity be kept undefiled.

Finally, no Christian can serve two masters, the Jehovah of the "Old Testament" and the God of the "New." More than that; no Christian, however sentimental or charitably disposed, can imbibe the poisoned teachings of Jehovah and remain a Christian. The two are diametrically opposed and cancel each other out.

Thus, writing to the notorious Karl Marx, Baruch Levy said:

"The Jewish people, taken collectively, will be its own Messiah. The Governors of the Jewish Race will administer in all places the public wealth. This will be realised by the promise of The Talmud that when the times of the Messiah come the Jews will hold under their keys the properties of all the peoples of the world."

What, then, is "The Talmud" that Levy quotes as his source for the foregoing prophecy? The Talmud is the Jewish Bible. It abhors the doctrine of the New Testament, denounces Christ and gloats over His crucifixion. It teaches hatred of Gentiles; to cheat and spurn them; to show them no mercy; to kill them. It consists of Rabbinical dissertations of 6,000 pages of commentaries on the Old Testament, all opposed to Christianity.

There is no reason why the Jews should not have their own faith. But why do Christians have to absorb so much of their doctrine, especially in the arena of Ethics, Economics and Finance when, according to *The Jewish World* (March, 1923), "Fundamentally Judaism is anti-Christian"; and according to the *Jewish Chronicle* (August 4th, 1919), "The ideals of Bolshevism at many points are consonant with the finest ideals of Judaism"?

If it is difficult to understand why non-Roman Catholics should be subjected to such indoctrination at the hands of ignorant or careless teachers, it is quite impossible to understand the same situation with Roman Catholics. Because Pope Gregory IX condemned The Talmud in these words: "It contains every kind of vileness and blasphemy against Christian truth."

Consider these few excerpts taken from The Talmud itself:

(1) Non-Jews are created to serve Jews.

(2) A Jew may be a hypocrite to a non-Jew.

(3) To despoil a non-Jew is permitted.

(4) God has ordained that the Jew shall take usury from the non-Jew.

(5) The best of the non-Jews should be exterminated. The honest life of the Gentile should be an object to hate.

(6) If a Jew can deceive a Gentile by pretending to be a non-Jew he is permitted to do so.

Despite the almost pathological vindictiveness of the above, Rabbi Lewis in his book, *Stranger than Fiction*, writes; "...the Jews lifted it (The Talmud) to a place of importance above the Bible."

Can it really be wondered at that a race brought up on such tenets have earned for themselves through all the centuries the dislike and distrust of their neighbours and hosts? People who hate are usually hated, and whether hate is openly expressed or not, the mental soil is greedy for growth.

In 1242, formal accusations were made against The Talmud by Pope Gregory IX, charging it with "blasphemies against God, against Jesus and against Christianity." The Pope appointed a Commission to examine the charges.

The Jews were represented by Jehiel, son of Joseph of Paris, and three others. The Commission sustained the charges and ordered the Talmud to be burnt. Twenty-four cart-loads were committed to the fire in Paris. In 1247 at the solicitation of the Jews the case was reopened but The Talmud was condemned again. (*History of the Jewish People*, P.378). The Talmud was also condemned and destroyed in Spain in 1415 and in Italy, 1559, (Ibid). But The Talmud's teachings, expressing the Judaic philosophy that now finds its flowering in Communism, that "unweeded garden" full of "things rank and gross in nature," remain in all their baleful growth: and THE PLAN, decried by Jews and sentimentalists alike as a "forgery" despite the obvious evidence of daily fulfilment, is their overall strategy of conquest.

Everything possible is done to keep Christians from learning the truth concerning The Talmud. If Christendom learned that, the Zionists would lose support of the very people whose protection they exploit in order to sow the fallacies of The Talmud in the minds of unsuspecting Christians. Because Zionists talk of God, Christians comfort themselves erroneously believing that the Talmudian god is the same as the Christian God. Nothing could be further from the truth, nor more dangerous to it, nor to Christianity.

Just consider this:

"Destruction of the Christian Church is fundamental to the aim of Judaism to secure world domination." Protocol 17.

"Our kingdom will be an apologia of the divinity Vishnu, in whom is found its personification. In our hundred hands will be, one in each, the springs of the machinery of social life." Protocol 17.

And:

"The King of the Jews will be the real Pope of the Universe." Protocol 17.

Those who launched The Plan for Zionist world domination did not see what their obsession would lead to, what it is leading to. Nor do the timely warnings of their fellow Jews who have seen the abyss to which these vile doctrines of hate and division are driving their race give the fanatical Zionists pause. In vain does Dr. Oscar Levy plead:

"We have erred my friends, we have erred...we who have posed as saviours of the world are to-day nothing but its seducers, its destroyers, its incendiaries, its executioners... and it is just our morality which has prohibited real progress... the day of reckoning is near. It will pass judgement upon our ancient faith."

In vain does left-wing publisher, Victor Gollancz, father of the notorious "Yellow Books" of the war admonish:

"The Jews must accept what they have rejected 2,000 years ago. They must accept whole-heartedly the Christian ethic."

We do not accept the thesis, urged upon us, that these wise warnings are merely part of the satanic guile of Zionist plotting.

Rather do we believe that if the Christian Church shook off its lethargy (which it prefers to call "tolerance") and spoke out "loud and clear" for its faith, multitudes of misled Jews would scorn what they now blindly follow.

There can be only one grim outcome to this warfare, cold or hot, open or hidden, between Zionism and Christianity; between Jehovah and God. It must result in the long dark night of despair, when the Four Horsemen will ride forth again. Unless Militant Christianity awakens in time to the test and the challenge.

For challenge there is and test there may be yet. Here, for instance, is only one small cloud, no bigger than a man's hand. Listen to Benjamin Freedman of New York:

"Soviet Communism will succeed in its attempt to conquer the world in direct proportion to the support which America gives to Zionism. This may sound startling but it is grimly true."

Have we not seen that grim warning fulfilled more than once since it was first uttered in 1947? Have we not heard the sickening clamour of America's Zionists and their Gentile dupes again and again in our ears since we forced open the gates of Belsen with the bloody hand of our national sacrifice? Have we not seen our great empire sold by fools to placate knaves, and all at the behest of Zionists in America? Do we not see it even now, again and again? Is not the warning in Protocol 15 timely for all Christendom? Ponder it now.

Talking of the Bolshevist revolution still to begin, THE PLAN laid down:

"The Russian Aristocracy, the one and only serious foe we have in the world, without counting the Papacy."

Why only the Russian Aristocracy, now butchered or scattered? Why only the Papacy? Is the U.S.A. impotent; or even the remaining might of this land and her sister states, proved in two world wars?

No, not impotent in might, but paralysed in understanding and will. For all the Zionists and their sympathisers have to do in the English-speaking countries is to raise the ancient cry of "witch hunt," even in the face of the most brazen treachery and betrayal, to halt all prosecutions and even all enquiries. While all the time Zionism working ruthlessly to its PLAN and through Communism, its tempered weapon, prepares for Armageddon, the last great battle of all, when the anti-Christ will make its final bid for the world's dominion in the overthrow of Christianity.

That is the stark issue. How we face it, we who are of Christian faith, will decide the outcome. Upon every man's decision now, rests his own personal and immortal fate. For upon his decision each man shall answer the question, for or against: MUST CHRIST (TRUTH) BE CRUCIFIED ANEW? This time with the connivance and co-operation of Christians.

Appendix 1. The author's obituary from *Candour*

DEATH OF "JOCK" CREAGH SCOTT

We record with profound regret the death of Lieut-Col. J. Creagh Scott, D.S.O., O.B.E., a member of the Council of *Candour*.

In the early days, when we had great difficulty in securing sponsors for our movement because most supporters were holding back, "Jock" Creagh Scott, without a moment's hesitation, gave us the use of his name and reputation. His support was absolutely invaluable. As he showed superb physical courage on the battlefields of the First World War, so in the undeclared war in which we are now engaged "Jock" always displayed a superb moral courage.

Colonel Creagh Scott had many other interests, especially in the West Country, but none was nearer to his heart than the *Candour*-League of Empire Loyalists movement. He did not always agree with the editor of this journal, but after stating his disagreement he invariably stood by decisions which went against him.

A determined fighter, his place in the leadership of the movement is irreplaceable. May this most courageous warrior rest in peace.

Candour # 216, 13th December 1957.

Suggested Further Reading

The Secret World Government by Major General, Count Cherep-Spiridovich

The Nameless War by Captain A.H.M. Ramsay

The New Unhappy Lords by A.K. Chesterton

Germany and England by Nesta Webster

Secret Societies and Subversive Movements by Nesta Webster

The Protocols as translated by Victor E. Marsden

The History of the League of Empire Loyalists and Candour by Hugh McNeile & Rob Black

The Morgethau Plan by David Irving

Hitler's War by David Irving

The Life of an American Jew in Israel by Jack Bernstein

The Synagogue of Satan by Andrew Carrington Hitchcock

The Israel Deception by David Lance Dean

Debating the Holocaust by Thomas Dalton

Pastor Charles Taze Russell by David Horowitz

The Occult Establishment by James Webb

Jewish Supremacism: My Awakening to the Jewish Question by David Duke

About The A.K. Chesterton Trust

The A.K. Chesterton Trust was formed by Colin Todd and the late Miss. Rosine de Bounevialle in January 1996 to succeed and continue the work of the now defunct Candour Publishing Co.

The objects of the Trust are stated as follows:

"To promote and expound the principles of A.K. Chesterton which are defined as being to demonstrate the power of, and to combat the power of International Finance, and to promote the National Sovereignty of the British World."

Our aims include:

- *Maintaining and expanding the range of material relevant to A.K. Chesterton and his associates throughout his life.*

- *To preserve and keep in-print important works on British Nationalism in order to educate the current generation of our people.*

- *The maintenance and recovery of the sovereign independence of the British Peoples throughout the world.*

- *The strengthening of the spiritual and material bonds between the British Peoples throughout the world.*

- *The resurgence at home and abroad of the British spirit.*

We will raise funds by way of merchandising and donations.

We ask that our friends make provision for *The A.K. Chesterton Trust* in their will.

The A.K. Chesterton Trust has a **duty** to keep *Candour* in the ring and punching.

CANDOUR: To defend national sovereignty against the menace of international finance.

CANDOUR: To serve as a link between Britons all over the world in protest against the surrender of their world heritage.

Subscribe to Candour

CANDOUR SUBSCRIPTION RATES FOR 10 ISSUES.

U.K. £30.00
Europe 50 Euros.
Rest of the World £45.00.
USA $60.00.

All Airmail. Cheques and Postal Orders, £'s Sterling only, made payable to *The A.K. Chesterton Trust*. (Others, please send cash by **secure post**, $ bills or Euro notes.)

Payment by Paypal is available. Please see our website **www.candour.org.uk** for more information.

Candour Back Issues

Back issues are available. 1953 to the present.

Please request our back issue catalogue by sending your name and address with two 1st class stamps to:

The A.K. Chesterton Trust, BM Candour, London, WC1N 3XX, UK

Alternatively, see our website at **www.candour.org.uk** where you can order a growing selection on-line.

British Peoples League

Britons Unite Worldwide

Box 691, Minden, Ontario. K0M 2K0, Canada.

www.britishpeoplesleague.com

Broadsword

The official supporting publication of the British Movement

For a sample copy of their 24-page Journal send £2.00 payable to *Broadsword* at:

PO Box 6, Heckmondwicke, WF16 0XF, England

Heritage and Destiny

Nationalist News & Views

For a sample copy of Heritage & Destiny, please send £5.00 payable to the same at:
40 Birkett Drive, Preston, PR2 6HE, England

The London Forum

The London Forum hosts regular meetings in Central London on a Pan-Nationalist theme with a wide range of speakers from across Europe and the World.

For more information please email: jezenglish@yahoo.co.uk

The A.K. Chesterton Trust Reprint Series

1. Creed of a Fascist Revolutionary & Why I Left Mosley - A.K. Chesterton.

2. The Menace of World Government & Britain's Graveyard - A.K. Chesterton.

3. What You Should Know About The United Nations - The League of Empire Loyalists.

4. The Menace of the Money-Power - A.K. Chesterton.

5. The Case for Economic Nationalism - John Tyndall.

6. Sound the Alarm! - A.K. Chesterton.

7. Six Principles of British Nationalism - John Tyndall.

8. B.B.C. - A National Menace - A.K. Chesterton.

9. Stand by the Empire - A.K. Chesterton.

10. Tomorrow. A Plan for the British Future - A.K. Chesterton.

11. The British Constitution and the Corruption of Parliament - Ben Greene.

12. Very High Finance & The Policy of a Patriot - Cahill & Strasser.

Other Titles from *The A.K. Chesterton Trust*

Leopard Valley - A.K. Chesterton.

Juma The Great - A.K. Chesterton.

The New Unhappy Lords - A.K. Chesterton.

Facing The Abyss - A.K. Chesterton.

The History of the League of Empire Loyalists - McNeile & Black

The A.B.C. of Politics - by Rosine de Bounevialle

All the above titles are available from The A.K. Chesterton Trust, BM Candour, London, WC1N 3XX, UK

www.candour.org.uk